Expansionism in International Human Rights Law

Brill Research Perspectives in International Legal Theory and Practice

Volumes published in this Brill Research Perspective are listed at *brill.com/rplts*

Expansionism in International Human Rights Law

By

Işıl Aral and Jean d'Aspremont

BRILL

LEIDEN | BOSTON

Library of Congress Control Number: 2024931439

Typeface for the Latin, Greek, and Cyrillic scripts: "Brill". See and download: brill.com/brill-typeface.

ISSN 2452-204X
ISBN 978-90-04-69607-5 (paperback)
ISBN 978-90-04-69608-2 (e-book)
DOI 10.1163/9789004696082

This book is printed on acid-free paper and produced in a sustainable manner.

Contents

Expansionism in International Human Rights Law

Işıl Aral and Jean d'Aspremont

Abstract

This book explores a specific discursivity at work in international human rights law. It examines the ways in which the discourse on international human rights law constantly expands its domain while preserving its distinctiveness from general international law. It particularly exposes the oscillations between generalist and exceptionalist claims made in international human rights law for the sake of expanding its scope. Reviewing several contemporary controversies on international human rights law, it sheds lights on the possible drivers behind such expansionist discursivity.

Keywords

discursivity – generalism – exceptionalism – law-ascertainment – interpretation – rhetorical power – positivisation of human rights – fragmentation – succession – termination of treaties – reservations – managerialism

Introduction

Human rights constitute an omnipresent discourse in domestic and global affairs. It is a discourse that has surpassed the borders of legal discourse and has become part of everyday life in some parts of the world. In that sense, human rights can no longer be reduced to just a legal entitlement determined through binding international law instruments and implemented by international institutions, bodies and courts. It is mobilized in almost every crisis and whenever anything related to individual, collective and environmental interests can be verbalized through the human rights vocabulary. While, for some, human rights have become yet another project to achieve justice,[1]

1 Samuel Moyn, *The Last Utopia: Human Rights in History* (Harvard University Press 2012).

 | DOI:10.1163/9789004696082_002

for others human rights are the *raison d'être* of any political community.[2] Irrespective of the dramatic setbacks witnessed in terms of compliance, there is no doubt that human rights, as a discourse, have expanded their scope, relevance, outreach, and symbolic capital to an unprecedented extent.

To become such a ubiquitous discourse, human rights have had to consolidate their scope, relevance, outreach, and symbolic capital within all the specific fields in which they are already rooted. This is the case in international law. Indeed, international human rights law have now secured a place in almost any debate about international law and global governance. There is hardly an international legal claim that cannot be configured and designed around a rule of international human rights law. With an emphasis on the modes of ascertainment of new rules of international human rights law, this monograph sheds light on some of those expansionist moves that enable international human rights law to constitute the seat of almost any claim on global affairs.[3] It particularly looks at the specific type of discursivity that has emerged in relation to international human rights law whereby the latter simultaneously anchors itself in general international law while ensuring it remains very distinct from it.

This book is structured as follows. Chapter 1 sets the stage for the discussion, introduces some of the main concepts on which the inquiry draws, and spells out the argument in further details. Chapter 2, drawing on the metaphor of international human rights law as an ever-expanding discourse, provides a short overview of the positivisation process of human rights in international law in the 20th century and discusses why international law came to be considered a fertile land for the positivisation of human rights. It then examines the ambiguity that has permeated the grounding of human rights in international law and especially the claims that international human rights law is both grounded in international law – which corresponds to a generalist posture – and distinct from it – which corresponds to an exceptionalist posture. Chapter 3 illustrates how the international legal discourse has oscillated between exceptionalist and generalist claims. First, it examines generalist claims to show how the expansionist discursivity tries to preserve its link to general international law by constantly falling back on general rules and principles of international law. Second, it turns to exceptionalist claims to demonstrate what kind of innovative manoeuvres have been witnessed in the discourse in order to detach human rights from general international law. Chapter 4 examines the

2 Costas Douzinas, *The End of Human Rights: Critical Thought at the Turn of the Century* (Oxford University Press 2000) 374.

3 On the sources of international human rights law, see Samantha Besson, 'Theorizing the Sources of International Law', in Samantha Besson and John Tasioulas (eds.), *The Philosophy of International Law* (Oxford University Press 2010).

emancipatory moves conducted with respect to sources of international law in order to evidence how international customary law, general principles of law, and soft law have been interpreted with great liberty when it comes to international human rights law. It further analyses other source-based expansionists moves that have been prevalent in this special regime. Chapter 5 explores the possible drivers behind the expansionist discursivity of international human rights law and investigates what might be the reasons that informed the deployment, in the legal discourse, of new expansionist discursive moves.

1 The Discursive Expansionism of International Human Rights Law

1.1 *Introductory Remarks and Main Concepts*

This book examines those expansionist moves geared towards the finding and ascertainment of *new* rules of international human rights law. It accordingly leaves aside argumentative manoeuvres and constructions aimed at substantiating the scope and content of existing rules. For the sake of delineating the object of this book, the identification of new international legal rules through law-ascertainment which this book focuses on must be distinguished from the expansion of the content of these rules through interpretation.[4] Indeed, this book grapples with the modes of law-ascertainment that allows the finding of new rules of international human rights law and turns a blind eye to the modes of content-determination that enables a substantiation of existing rules of international human rights law.

It is important to stress at this stage that modes of law-ascertainment discussed here should not be reduced to technical devices. Both the identification of new rules of international human rights law at the heart of this volume and the interpretation of the content of existing rules which are not looked at here are interpretive processes where law, facts, their relations are continuously being created.[5] In that sense, both processes are hermeneutical, definitional and delineating in nature. That being said, the focus of this monograph is solely on modes of law-ascertainment techniques that are used in international human rights law for the sake of the latter's expansionism.

4 Jean d'Aspremont, *Formalism and the Sources of International Law: A Theory of the Ascertainment of Legal Rules* (Oxford University Press 2011) 157–61. See also Jean d'Aspremont, 'The Multidimensional Process of Interpretation: Content-Determination and Law-Ascertainment Distinguished' in Andrea Bianchi, Daniel Peat, and Matthew Windsor (eds.), *Interpretation in International Law* (Oxford University Press 2015) 111–29.

5 d'Aspremont, 'The Multidimensional Process of Interpretation: Content-Determination and Law-Ascertainment Distinguished' (n 4) 117.

The idea of expansion also warrants some definitional observations. Expansion is primarily a spatial notion that refers to the capture or apprehension of new terrains beyond an original position in space. In that respect, expansion presupposes a fixed spatial configuration. Expansion also is a reifying notion in that it presupposes that both the original position as well as the gains acquired through expansions have some kind of material existence. For the sake of this book, it is of the utmost importance to stress that expansionism carries neither this spatial nor reifying dimension. Indeed, this book is premised on the idea that international human rights law is a discourse that has no material existence other than in the texts in which it is verbalized. In other words, international human rights law is not a thing whose state or size is increased or inflated by virtue of the expansionism discussed in the following chapters. What is at stake here is how international human rights law, as discourse, allows new claims about global affairs and a new ordering of the world.

The notion of human rights discourse with which this book engages warrants an additional definitional observation. A discourse is understood here in a rather generic way as to refer to any system of meaning and set of connected utterances through which one speaks about and come to experience the world and human phenomena.[6] In the more specific context of this book, the notion of discourse allows the following engagement with the expansionism of international human rights law to be reduced neither to fixed and exclusive structures nor to mere conscious and deliberate discursivity of actors. The discursive moves described in this book are events that are constantly re-enacted, re-written and re-invented by all those who contribute to contemporary legal thought and practice. In other words, the notion of discourse that is used throughout this book allows one to look simultaneously at the structures and the agents at work behind contemporary legal thought and practice related international human rights law.[7]

A final remark is in order. Expansionism, and thus the attempt to get hold on new objects of thought and meaning-making, is certainly not a feature

6 On the notion of discourse, see gen. Hayden White, *Tropics of Discourse: Essays in Cultural Criticism* (Johns Hopkins University Press 1978) 4–5. See also Michel Foucault, *Dits et écrits, I* (1954–1975) (Gallimard 2001) 623. On the idea that a discourse does violence to things, see Michel Foucault, *L'ordre du Discours* (Gallimard 1971) 55.

7 See the famous charge of Bourdieu against the idea of structure and the idea that structuralists do not take into account the social conditions of productions of language, see Pierre Bourdieu, *Ce que Parler Veut Dire: L'économie des Echanges Linguistiques* (Fayard 1982) 7–9. See also the criticisms by Michel Foucault, *Dits et écrits, Tome 2* (Gallimard 2001) 145, 1254. See also David W Kennedy, 'Critical Theory, Structuralism and Contemporary Legal Scholarship' (1985–1986) 21 New England Law Review 209, 249.

specific to international human rights law. Most discourses, for they are ways to speak about the world, give it meaning, and organize it, constantly seek to conquer new terrains of thought and of meaning-making. Said differently, most discourses are driven by the perpetual *production of new discursive materials*[8] which are then immediately captured, organized, and ordered by the discourse concerned.[9] One of these technologies[10] which discourses resort to with a view to producing new discursive materials and ordering them is expansionism. International human rights law is no exception to that. This is also a feature of the expansionism witnessed in international human rights law.[11]

1.2 *International Human Rights Law: Then and Now*

International human rights law started to develop systematically after the establishment of the United Nations in 1945.[12] International law, at the time,

---

8 Comp. with the idea of over-production of knowledge for the sake of ordering. see Michel Foucault, *Dits et Ecrits, II* (Gallimard 2001) 554–555. See also the idea of discursive eruption ('explosion discursive') see Michel Foucault, *Histoire de la Sexualité 1: La Volonté de Savoir* (Gallimard 1976) at 25. The way in which an economy of secret serves a specific discourse ordering through an outpouring of discourse is at the heart of Michel Foucault's first volume on the history of sexuality. See gen. Michel Foucault, *Histoire de la Sexualité 1: La Volonté de Savoir* (Gallimard 1976), esp. 33, 48–49.

9 Foucault (n 8) 48–49, Foucault, *Dits et Ecrits, II* (n 8) 248. On the idea of distinctions and binary categories as powerful modes of ordering, see Gilles Deleuze and Claire Parnet, *Dialogues* (Champs Essais 1996) 29, Roland Barthes, *Leçon* (Seuil 1978) 12, Bruno Latour, *Nous n'avons Jamais Eté Modernes : Essai d'Anthropologie Symétrique* (La Découverte 1997) 68–69, Michel Foucault, Les Mots et les Choses (Gallimard 1966) 68–69. On the idea that thoughts classify and thus order, see Michel Foucault, Naissance de la Clinique (PUF 1963) 27.

10 In the contemporary literature, the concept of discursive technology is most of the time associated with the deployment of advanced technological tools, see Jay Lemke, 'Discursive Technologies and the Social Organization of Meaning', (2001) 35 Folia Linguistica, 79–96, Eran Fisher, *Media and New Capitalism in the Digital Age* (Palgrave Macmillan 2010) chapter 2, Marie-Anne Paveau, 'Réalité et Discursivité: D'autres Dimensions pour la Théorie Du Discours' (2012) 34 Semen 95–115, Marie-Anne, Paveau, 'Les Prédiscours: Sens, Mémoire, Cognition, (2006) Presses Sorbonne Nouvelle 132. Here the notion is used to refer to a non-material and non-textual device or technique of a cultural, cognitive, or intellectual nature that governs the speaking and the thinking in a given environment and in a given group of interlocutors. It is thus a device that produces specific attitudes, presumptions, needs, and experiences to any user of the discourse. On this understanding of discursive technology, see Michel Foucault, Sécurité, Territoire, Population: Cours au Collège de France, 1977–1978 (Gallimard 2004) 128–134, 151–169, Foucault, Histoire de la Sexualité 1: La Volonté de Savoir (n 11) 78–91, Foucault, Dits et Ecrits, II (n 8) 548–566, 956–958, Michel Foucault, *Dits et Ecrits, II* (Gallimard 2001) 566, 587, 958, 1013.

11 See infra chapter 5, section 1.

12 See infra section 2.1.

was aimed at protecting certain minimal standards by making them part of the existing international legal order. By turning moral values into rights and making them binding on states, it was thought that the protection of the individual would be guaranteed through international law. What is called the human rights expansionist discourse for the purposes of this monograph refers to the tendency of the legal discourse on human rights to craft a niche for human rights within general international law. The positivisation of human rights law started by an endeavour to find a favourable location for this new set of rules within an already existing legal framework. For those who wanted to anchor the protection of fundamental rights into international law, this endeavour did not only consist of creating an additional regime of international law where the same discursive constructions would apply. Rather than making human rights a sub-field of international law, it was more favourable to both benefit from the discursive constructions that already existed in international law but also to create new tools to expand it. When human rights law is considered a special regime of international law, it is often insinuated that it is a sub-field of international law with its own distinct rules. The human rights expansionist discourse, however, is used here to refer to the expansionism at work in the human rights legal discourse through the constant discursive oscillation between exceptionalist and generalist claims witnessed therein. Thus, for the sake of this book, the human rights expansionist discourse constitute a discursive phenomenon which consists of new discursive constructions and new arguments which are not fully stable for they constantly seesaw between generalist claims and exceptionalist claims but which all aim at ensuring that human rights are the seats of most claims on global affairs.

Since its inception, international human rights law – which, as was said, is a feature of most discourses –[13] has been articulated around an expansionist discursivity which has been implemented by the simultaneous grounding of human rights in international law and the firm distinction between the former and the latter. This is why the legal discourse has constantly been a site of claims foregrounding the exceptional character of human rights obligations, the non-reciprocal nature of these obligations, their constitutional character, the idea that different rules that should be applied to international human rights treaties, in particular regarding breaches of obligations, reservations, standing, succession and withdrawal. These are only some of the constructions and claims which have been witnessed in the legal discourse and that have been at the service of an expansion of international human rights law. Through some creative moves, it has been claimed that the nature of human

13 See supra section 1.1.

rights obligations requires different discursive constructions than those which are used in general international law.[14] This favoured the expansion of human rights law through the creation of new rules by making adjustments to discursive moves employed in general international law. It can even be argued that this expansionist inclination is at the heart of the human rights discourse which constantly tries to break away with the rigid discursive moves that have been associated with general international law. The space occupied by human rights law within general international law has been expanded by underlining the special nature of human rights. It has been frequently argued by those involved in human rights law that although general international law provides the premises for the development of human rights law as a special regime, the former needs to be tailored in order to meet the demands of the latter. To that end, the legal discourse has generously and widely accommodated exceptionalist claims which emphasise how human rights law requires different discursive moves than general international law.

These exceptionalist claims are an efficient tool to expand the scope of human rights law. This does not mean, however, that the legal discourse has simultaneously enabled a total rupture from general international law. Indeed, the expansionism of the human rights discourse has not been concomitant with a total emancipation from general international law. Whenever the legal categories created specifically for international human rights law will not suffice, recourse will necessarily be made to general international law.[15] Rather than designing this new legal order as an autonomous or self-contained regime, the discourse constantly stresses the kinship between the two legal orders. It was frequently emphasised by judges of international courts, human rights scholars or international organisations that human rights law is closely attached to general international law. The expansionist discursivity tries on one hand to tailor international law to meet the demands of human rights but on the other hand any fundamental difference that would cause a total

14 Lea Brilmayer, 'From "Contract" to "Pledge": The Structure of International Human Rights Agreements', (2006) Yale Law School, Faculty Scholarship Series, Paper 3753, Rosalyn Higgins, *Problems and Process* (Oxford University Press 1994) 95–96. For a criticism of the special nature of international human rights law, see Matthew Craven, 'Legal Differentiation and the Concept of the Human Rights Treaty in International Law' (2000) 11 European Journal of International Law 489–519.

15 Fragmentation of International Law: Difficulties Arising from the Diversification and Expansion of International', Report of the Study Group of the International Law Commission, Finalized by Martti Koskenniemi, UN Doc A/CN.4/L.682 (13 April 2006), para. 152. It is because international human rights law is not an autonomous regime totally emancipated from general international law that the ILC preferred to use the term 'special regime', rather than 'self-contained', see ibid.

rupture is eliminated. International human rights law cannot be completely isolated from general international law. This monograph examines how this oscillation between exceptionalist claims whereby international human rights law departs from general international law and generalist claims whereby it anchors itself to general international law serves a discursivity that helps to expand international human rights law.

It is important to emphasise that when reference is made to international human rights law, it does not imply the existence of a single, homogenous set of human rights standards. Rather, international human rights framework is a complex set of obligations created through not only treaty or customary law, but also universal and regional mechanisms including mainly the United Nations, the Council of Europe, the African Union and the Organization of American States. International human rights consist of various sets of heterogenous rules that are interconnected and overlapping, opposing, diverging. The human rights obligations that international law actors create contradict, confirm, expand or disregard one another in various ways. In that sense, it is not possible to talk about a special human rights regime that is separate from international law that forms a harmonious set of rules and processes. International human rights law is used here to indicate international law norms that aim to protect the interests of individuals.

1.3 *The Relationship between International Human Rights Law and General International Law*

For it constitutes a key insight for the elucidation of how expansionism plays out in international human rights law, the relationship between the latter and general international law warrants a few observations. Such relationship can be investigated from various angles. And it has been so over the last decades. In the 1980s, when international human rights law expanded at an exponential rate, the relationship of human rights with general international law became the object of much debate. The first wave of research conducted into the relationship between these two regimes aimed at grasping the impact that the growing body of human rights corpus would have on general international law and how it would change the way we understand both fields. Alston opined that human rights law separated itself from general international law to acquire the ability to detach itself from discursive moves that might hinder its development.[16] He argued that human rights lawyers were trying to tailor

16 Philip Alston, 'Making Space for New Human Rights: The Case of the Right to Development', (1988) 1 Harvard Human Rights Yearbook 3, 12.

general international law to meet their own policy choices.[17] When Simma was examining the relationship between human rights and international law, he claimed that there was no conceptual endeavour to explain what human rights are, and that most attempts trying to grasp this new field were merely descriptive.[18] It is noteworthy that at the time he recognised how on one hand human rights were gradually detaching from general international law while still keeping its attachment to it. He stated that '[w]hen isolated rules, principles and treaties grow into a field, or regime, of their own, there seems to develop an unavoidable tendency on the part of the scholarship engaged in the field to somehow "de-couple" itself from the body of general theory on which it is (and remains) based.'[19] Simma drew attention to the growing body of human rights treaties and increasing number of international institutions dealing with human rights problems.[20] Considering the ever-expanding nature of human rights law, he inquired how sources of international law manifest special characteristics in human rights law. He examined how modes of reasoning in human rights treaties, customs and general principles of law and also soft law differ from the modes of reasoning in general international law. His endeavour was mostly geared towards mapping out areas where human rights law and international law converge and diverge in the application of sources.

The second wave of research conducted into the relationship between general international law and international human rights law has focused on the harmonisation of these two fields. The famous report of the International Law Commission detailed at length the proliferation of separate normative systems in international law which co-exist with their own rules, processes, institutions, principles, monitoring and dispute resolution mechanisms.[21] International

17 Ibid 12.

18 Bruno Simma, 'International Human Rights and General International Law' in *Collected Courses of the Academy of the European Union Law, Vol. IV 2* (Martinus Nijhoff Publishers 1993) 164.

19 Ibid 164.

20 Ibid 153.

21 See 'Fragmentation of International Law: Difficulties Arising from the Diversification and Expansion of International', Report of the Study Group of the International Law Commission, Finalized by Martti Koskenniemi, UN Doc A/CN.4/L.682 (13 April 2006). On general international law as a legal system, see Anastasios Gourgourinis, 'General/Particular International Law and Primary/Secondary Rules: Unitary Terminology of a Fragmented System', (2011) 22 European Journal of International Law 993–1026. On the concept of unity, see Mario Prost, *The Concept of Unity in Public International Law* (Bloomsbury Publishing 2012). On the impact of fragmentation regarding the systematicity of international law, see Liam Murphy, *What Makes Law: An Introduction to the Philosophy of Law* (Cambridge University Press 2014) 152–157. On the fragmentation of international human rights law see, Eva Brems, 'Should Pluriform Human Rights Become One? Exploring the

human rights law is not the only field where new discursive moves have been created. General international law has expanded into several distinct fields with their own problems, solutions, institutions, monitoring bodies, rules and discursive constructions which at times can create contradictory outcomes.[22] International humanitarian law, law of the sea, international economic law, international refugee law, international environmental law are only some examples of different legal orders which move away from general international law in several aspects. The creation of different discursive moves for each of these legal orders can at times bring about contradictory solutions to similar disputes. The ILC report is premised on the idea that international law does not promote conflict among different normative regimes.[23] International actors, whenever they commit to new international obligations, do not intent to take on conflicting obligations. In that sense, the ILC searched for ways to reduce the tension between different legal regimes.

The fragmentation of international law can be told as a positive narrative that refers to the diversity of the discipline or it can equally be presented as a negative narrative that tells a story of underdevelopment.[24] When the relationship between international human rights law and general international law is construed as one of fragmentation, this implies that the development of a special regime within international law poses a threat to the unity of the field.[25] The fragmentation report of the ILC problematises the coherence of international law. It examines the relationship between special regimes and general international law to understand how the normative conflict is created and what it tells us about the unity of the discipline. In that sense, it is

---

Benefits of Human Rights Integration', (2014) European Journal of Human Rights 447–70, Marjan Ajevski, 'Fragmentation in International Human Rights Law – Beyond Conflict of Laws', (2014) 32 Nordic Journal of Human Rights 87–98, Mehrdad Payandeh, 'Fragmentation within International Human Rights Law' in Mads Tønnesson Andenæs and Eirik Bjorge (eds.), *A Farewell to Fragmentation* (Cambridge University Press 2015).

22 Anja Lindroos, 'Addressing Norm Conflicts in a Fragmented Legal System: The Doctrine of Lex Specialis', (2005) 74 Nordic Journal of International Law 27–66, 31.

23 Fragmentation of International Law: Difficulties Arising from the Diversification and Expansion of International', Report of the Study Group of the International Law Commission, Finalized by Martti Koskenniemi, UN Doc A/CN.4/L.682 (13 April 2006), para. 37.

24 Anne-Charlotte Martineau, 'The Rhetoric of Fragmentation: Fear and Faith in International Law', (2009) 22 Leiden Journal of International Law 1–28.

25 Martti Koskenniemi and Päivi Leino, 'Fragmentation of International Law? Postmodern Anxieties', (2002) 15 Leiden Journal of International Law 553–79, Bruno Simma, 'Universality of International Law from the Perspective of a Practitioner', (2009) 20 European Journal of International Law 265–97, 267. See also, Prost, *The Concept of Unity in Public International Law* (n 21).

concerned with the conflict of norms when there are two regimes with conflicting rules and principles. It further analyses the tools such as *jus cogens, erga omnes, lex specialis, lex generalis* and how they can help to overcome legal uncertainty that might be caused due to conflict of norms. In that sense, it can be argued that the approach of the ILC construes the relationship between international human rights law and general international law as a relationship of potential conflicts and looked for argumentative techniques and principles to overcome them in order to enhance the coordination between the two regimes.

Another investigation regarding the relationship between international human rights law and general international law has concentrated on the impact of the former on the latter. The research conducted by the International Law Association examined how the development of international human rights law challenged some well-established mechanisms of general international law.[26] It concentrated on selected legal issues that have been substantially developed through international human rights law in order to protect individuals. They have assessed how these developments affected general international law by examining mainly the practice of the International Court of Justice and the work of the ILC. They have analysed to what extent these bodies referred to concepts that have been specifically generated by human rights bodies. The Committee on International Human Rights Law and Practice of the ILA which was tasked with making this assessment stated expressly that it was 'desirable' to witness how the development of human rights transformed general international law into a legal system that is less state-centred and more concerned with the problems of the individual.[27] As in the case of the fragmentation approach, the ILA was also preoccupied with addressing the coherence of international law and attempted to reconcile the two regimes.[28]

Meron's account concentrated on how the developments of human rights humanised general international law.[29] His approach was similar to the approach of ILA in the sense that he traced the impact of human rights and international humanitarian law on general international law to analyse the cross-fertilisation between different legal orders. He examined how human rights and international humanitarian law transformed several areas of general international law including law of war, sources, international criminal

26 Menno Kamminga and Martin Scheinin (eds.), *The Impact of Human Rights Law on General International Law* (Oxford University Press 2009).

27 Ibid 4.

28 Ibid 1–2.

29 Theodor Meron, *The Humanization of International Law* (Martinus Nijhoff Publishers 2006).

law, international courts and state responsibility. According to Sheeran, the relationship between the two legal orders is 'a complex narrative of tension, evolution and juxtaposition'.[30] In his examination of this relationship, he argued that international human rights will have to fall back on general international law when it is necessary and therefore cannot be considered a self-contained regime. He sustained that due to this inter-dependence, the relationship between the two regimes will always be marked by a certain tension which is unavoidable because of norm conflicts.[31]

What is common among the research already conducted about the relationship between international human rights law and general international law is that they all conceptualise this relationship based on a tension that needs to be resolved and remedied or a process of change and impact. International human rights law is projected as a field that stands at a certain opposition against general international law. It seems that the expansion of international human rights law with its different rules, processes, institutions and most importantly different discursive moves is an immense source of conflict. Even in cases where there is no conflict, the resort of international human rights law to different discursive moves generates a certain tension with general international law. In other words, the relationship is portrayed as one of crisis.

It goes without saying that international law thrives in crisis.[32] This does not mean, however, that any issue that deserves a closer look necessarily entails a conflict or disagreement that needs to be overcome. This monograph does not construe the relationship between international human rights law and general international law as a relationship of conflict, tension or crisis that requires to be remedied. It conceptualises the process of positivisation of human rights law as an expansionist discourse that is built on a constant oscillation between exceptionalist and generalist claims. On one hand, human rights law anchors itself into international law but on the other hand, it moves away from it by creating new discursive constructions. This constant oscillation provides the favourable space for human rights to expand its reach. This oscillation is used for an expansionist discursivity that might serve various purposes. This does not mean that it is necessarily good or bad for human rights to pursue this

30 Scott Sheeran, 'The Relationship of International Human Rights Law and General International Law: Hermeneutic Constraint, or Pushing the Boundaries' in Scott Sheeran and Nigel Rodley (eds.), *Routledge Handbook of International Human Rights Law* (Routledge 2014) 79.

31 Ibid 83.

32 Hilary Charlesworth, 'International Law: A Discipline of Crisis', (2002) 65 The Modern Law Review 377–92, Makane Moïse Mbengue and Jean d'Aspremont (eds.), *Crisis Narratives in International Law* (Brill 2021).

expansionist discursivity. In that sense, this study does not rely on a discourse of crisis, conflict or anxiety that should be examined, consumed and brought to a solution by international law.

The approach of this monograph differs from the existing accounts by not conceptualising the relationship between human rights law and general international law as one of conflict, underdevelopment, uncertainty, inconsistency or disharmony. The impetus here is not about harmonising, uniting or reconciling these two regimes. What this study seeks is not to find ways of unity for international law to function as a system of harmonious rules.[33] Rather, the aim here is to examine how creative ways of expanding human rights through new modes of law-ascertainment came to surface in the legal discourse. It thus understands international law as a creative space where new discursive constructions are floated, tested, mobilised, embraced and contested.[34]

The following chapters will particularly show that international human rights law comes with a specific discursivity whereby international human rights law tries to detach itself from general international law but at the same time strives to stay anchored into general international law. Exceptionalist claims pull human rights law away from general international law by emphasising the special nature of international protection that should be accorded to individuals. These exceptionalist claims which underline the special nature of human rights law and the generalist claims that support the kinship between the two orders work in tandem for an expansionist discursivity. This constant oscillation between exceptionalist and generalist claims help the expansionism of international human rights law which is at the heart of this expansionist discourse. In order to advance this argument, the monograph takes a closer look at the creation of the human rights law expansionist discourse, its endeavours, how in practice these manoeuvres are put into practice and the motivations behind the expansionist discursivity. The effort put into demonstrating the special character of human rights obligations has already been criticised in the scholarship.[35] It is not the aim of this monograph to review or to respond to these criticisms. Here, the focus is on the examination of the oscillation between exceptionalist claims whereby human rights

33 For a critique of the idea of unity and coherence in international law, see Jean d'Aspremont, 'The Chivalric Pursuit of Coherence in International Law", (2023) 36 Leiden Journal of International Law (forthcoming).

34 On the idea of texts as spaces, see Jean d'Aspremont, 'Two Attitudes toward Textuality in International Law: The Battle for Dualism', (2022) 42 Oxford Journal of Legal Studies 963–984.

35 Matthew Craven, 'Legal Differentiation and the Concept of the Human Rights Treaty in International Law', (2000) 11 European Journal of International Law 489–519.

law aims to detach itself from general international law and generalist claims whereby it anchors itself to it. The contrary, a total emancipation from general international law, would turn human rights into mere moral values without legal pedigree.[36] This would wipe out any authority that human rights can claim by anchoring itself into an international law framework. In that sense, it is necessary for human rights to ensure its attachment with the positive law order of international law in order to preserve its credibility and authority.

It is important to stress that the oscillation between exceptionalist and generalist claims examined in the following chapters do not necessarily create a relationship of conflict or uncertainty. This study is thus not interested in the harmonious functioning of international law, trying to enforce or deduce a regular pattern. It does not aim to streamline the two regimes and create a coordination between them. Rather it conceives these two fields as a rich source of discursive phenomena.

A final observation is in order. It must be recalled that legal language is a rich source of discursive power and is a vehicle of world-making.[37] It provides boundless sources for imaginative possibilities to anyone who wants to change, criticise, improve or remake the normative world they live in. It can even be argued that 'there is *nothing but* imagination' when one writes about international law.[38] In this normative world where there is no ultimate power to determine how we should interpret our surroundings, how we use the words at our disposal shapes the way we convey meaning.[39] International human rights law was shaped through the discursive moves of international law but moulded it in such a way that the new special regime was equipped with its own discursive constructions. International human rights law is a field marked by creativity and imagination.[40] The positivisation of human rights in international law and the creation of a new field based on general rules of international law showcased how the legal discourse can constantly re-invent itself and provide space for new discursive moves of an expansionist character.

---

36 Allen Buchanan, *The Heart of Human Rights* (Oxford University Press 2013) 11, Patrick Macklem, *The Sovereignty of Human Rights* (Oxford University Press 2015) 22.

37 James Boyd White, *The Legal Imagination* (University of Chicago Press 1985) xiii.

38 Gerry Simpson, 'Imagination' in Jean d'Aspremont and Sahib Singh (eds.), *Concepts for International Law: Contributions to Disciplinary Thought* (Edward Elgar 2019) 414.

39 Jean d'Aspremont, 'Wording in International Law', (2012) 25 Leiden Journal of International Law 575–602.

40 On the contrary, Koskenniemi argued that 'as international lawyers, we have failed to use the imaginative possibilities open to us' in Martti Koskenniemi, *From Apology to Utopia: The Structure of International Legal Argument* (Cambridge University Press 2006) 561.

By conceptualising international law as a creative discursive space, this study seeks to shed light on the power of imagination at work in the legal discourse and how new discursive constructions have emerged for the sake of expanding human rights law.

2 International Human Rights Law as an Ever-Expanding Discourse

This chapter aims to provide a short historical background of the positivisation process of human rights in order to explain how the protection of individual interests became an essential part of general international law. While the following chapters will elaborate on the innovative constructions that have been witnessed in the legal discourse in order to expand this special regime, it is essential to discuss why rather than a purely domestic protection, it was considered to be necessary to provide a second layer of protection to human rights at the international level. In that sense, it is important to explore why international law was considered a fertile land for the protection of human rights. This positivisation process was very soon followed by the creation of new discursive moves specific to human rights. This chapter endeavours to provide an overview of the process by which human rights was first made part of international law and then sheds light on the creation of new discursive moves specific to international human rights law.

At this preliminary stage, it must be emphasised that human rights have long been in the making. The idea that individuals should enjoy a certain minimal standard of living just by virtue of their humanity has deep historical, philosophical and political roots. The positivisation of human rights by transforming it into a topic that should be governed by international law is, however, a recent phenomenon. In international law, 'rights' were first created to protect the interests of states.[41] It is only in the aftermath of the Second World War, that questions about how rights could also be accorded to individuals started to emerge and be raised. It is to that end that the positivisation of rights paved the way for the human rights expansionist discourse. 'Rights' became not only a concept that protected the interests of states, but protected individuals as well.[42] Until the 20th century, it was not contested that states

41 Jean d'Aspremont, 'The Doctrine of Fundamental Rights of States and Anthropomorphic Thinking in International Law', (2015) 4 Cambridge International Law Journal 501–20.

42 On the historical evolution of rights, see Samuel Moyn, 'Rights' in d'Aspremont and Singh (eds.), *Concepts for International Law: Contributions to Disciplinary Thought* (Edward

were free to treat their citizens however they wished since it was a matter that was regarded to be strictly within the domestic jurisdiction of the state. The establishment of the United Nations played a key role in the transformation of human rights from mere moral values to part of positive law. In 1945, the United Nations took up the matter and became a generator of human rights standards. It is only after the United Nations established bodies to be tasked with the production of human rights norms and monitoring mechanisms that human rights started to become part of international law. International law provided a safe and favourable niche to human rights to develop and prosper.

When the human rights expansionist discourse started to take shape in the aftermath of the Second World War, claims about human rights were first grounded in international law which, allegedly, provided efficient tools to oblige states from above to respect fundamental rights.[43] It can be contended that human rights aim to force states to treat their citizens in accordance with certain minimal standards. This can be put into practice both at the domestic level through the incorporation of fundamental rights into the domestic legal framework but also at the international level by adopting multilateral human rights treaties and establishing international bodies and courts to monitor state compliance. It was the latter approach that dominated the legal discourse on human rights in the aftermath of 1945. International law was seen as a favourable legal system to give life to this newly developing field of law. Nevertheless, the human rights expansionist discourse had very distinctive aims that could hardly be realised by a loyal and mechanical attachment to the rules of general international law. Such discursive ambitions required to tailor general international law and create new discursive moves. To that end, they presented several justifications as to why this specific regime has to garner itself with specific rules. Before the following chapters elucidate how the human rights expansionist discourse is premised on an oscillation between exceptionalist and generalist claims, this chapter traces the positivisation of human rights in international law (2.1.), investigates why international law provided a fertile land for it to grow (2.2.), and finally examines why there was a necessity to differentiate human rights from general international law (2.3.).

2.1 *The Land Afar Becomes Close: The Positivisation of Human Rights*

The journey that human rights took over the years to gain its contemporary status has been told numerous times. It is possible to go back several centuries

---

Elgar 2019).

43 Frédéric Mégret, 'Nature of Obligations' in Daniel Moeckli et al. (eds.), *International Human Rights Law* (Oxford University Press 2014) 87.

back and find traces of human rights in any region of the world.[44] In that sense, the long story of human rights would have to travel all around the world to provide a holistic picture. On the other hand, the short story of human rights has been traditionally told by an emphasis on developments that took place in Western states. This Eurocentric story usually starts with a reference to Magna Carta as one of the earliest instances where a group of elites managed to convince the sovereign to grant them some protection against his unlimited power.[45] The example of Magna Carta is often followed by the adoption of the Habeas Corpus Act in 1679 and the Bill of Rights in 1689 in the UK – domestic documents that guaranteed the limitation of the king's power in favour of individuals for the protection of certain fundamental rights.[46] This short story of human rights is followed by the French Declaration of the Rights of Man and Citizen of 1789 which proclaimed in its preamble 'the natural, unalienable and sacred rights of man' and aimed at limiting the absolute power of the monarch. The American Declaration of Independence of 1776, which underlined that 'all men are created equal' with certain unalienable rights, is another instance which forms part of the classical Western-centric history of human rights. This development is followed by the 1776 Virginia Declaration of Rights which guaranteed that 'all men are by nature equally free and independent, and have inherent rights'. These are only some examples of domestic law documents that are often cited as the primary sources of inspiration for documents that have been adopted at the United Nations for the positivisation of human rights.[47] This classic story that takes place in Western states and culminates in the emergence of international human rights law in 1945 omits

---

44 See generally, Jacob Giltaij and Kaius Tuopi, 'Human rights in Antiquity? Revisiting Anachronism and Roman Law' in Pamela Slotte and Miia Halme (eds.), *Revisiting the Origins of Human Rights* (Cambridge University Press 2015), Richard Bauman, *Human Rights in Ancient Rome* (Routledge 2012), Robert Weatherley, *The Discourse of Human Rights in China: Historical and Ideological Perspectives* (Springer 1999), Jack Mahoney, *The Challenge of Human Rights: Origin, Development and Significance* (Wiley-Blackwell 2008), Micheline Ishay, *The History of Human Rights: From Ancient Times to the Globalization Era* (University of California Press 2008), Mashood Baderin, *International Human Rights and Islamic Law* (Oxford University Press 2003).

45 See Francesca Klug, *A Magna Carta for All Humanity: Homing in on Human Rights* (Routledge 2015).

46 Andrew Blick, *Beyond Magna Carta: A Constitution for the United Kingdom* (Oxford University Press 2015) 63–90.

47 On the impact of the Enlightenment era and the revolutions of the 18th century on the development of the idea of human rights, see Lynn Hunt, *Inventing Human Rights: A History* (W. W. Norton & Company 2008).

non-European experiences that address human dignity and puts limits to the absolute power of the sovereign.[48]

While there have been some developments in domestic law of Western states with regard to the protection of the individual against the unlimited power of the sovereign, individuals were not of an essential concern for international law until the 1940s. This does not mean, however, that there was no protection at all regarding individuals in international law before the 20th century. Diplomatic protection, for instance, has provided certain minimal guarantees.[49] The treatment of aliens is another forum where states were bound to provide some protection to individuals. Another prominent example of the protection provided to individuals in international law before the 20th century took shape with the positivisation of rules of international humanitarian law through first the Geneva Convention of 1864 and then the Hague Conventions of 1899 and 1907.[50] International treaties prohibiting slave trade can be cited as another instance of protection of a fundamental right in international law.[51] International Labour Organization was founded in 1919 under the Treaty of Versailles in order to establish international labour standards and protect the rights of workers.[52] It should finally be noted that these examples about the protection of individuals at the international level before the 1940s should be seen as sporadic developments, rather than part of a concerted effort.

Following these domestic regulations about fundamental rights in Western states, and sporadic developments such as the prohibition of slavery, the treaties

48 Anthony Anghie, 'International Human Rights Law and a Developing World Perspective' in Sheeran and Rodley (eds.), *Routledge Handbook of International Human Rights Law* (Routledge 2016) 111.

49 Annemarieke Vermeer-Künzli, 'Diplomatic Protection as a Source of Human Rights Law' in Dinah Shelton (ed.), *The Oxford Handbook of International Human Rights Law* (Oxford University Press 2013).

50 Mary Ellen O'Connell, 'Historical Developments and Legal Basis', in Dieter Fleck (ed.), *The Handbook of International Humanitarian Law* (Oxford University Press 2021). For a critical account of the humanitarian aspect of international humanitarian law, see David Kennedy, *The Dark Sides of Virtue: Reassessing International Humanitarianism* (Princeton University Press 2005), Chapter 8. On the recent history of international humanitarian law, see Boyd Van Dijk, *Preparing for War: The Making of the 1949 Geneva Conventions* (Oxford University Press 2022).

51 Jenny S Martinez, *The Slave Trade and the Origins of International Human Rights Law* (Oxford University Press 2011).

52 Gerry Rodgers et al., *The International Labour Organization and the Quest for Social Justice, 1919–2009* (International Labour Office 2009), Lee Swepston, 'The International Labour Organization and International Human rights System' in Sheeran and Rodley (eds.), *Routledge Handbook of International Human Rights Law* (Routledge 2016).

on international humanitarian law or the establishment of the International Labour Organization, the classical history posits the birth of human rights law as part of international law to the establishment of the United Nations. Until 1945, it can be argued that the protection of fundamental rights was not of a particular concern for international law. It is only after the establishment of the United Nations that there has been an essential transformation in the way fundamental rights have transformed into an issue to be regulated by international law.[53] Some scholars regarded the transposition of a state's obligations towards its nationals from domestic into international sphere as a necessity for the international peace. Lauterpacht, for instance, argued that unless international law regulated some form of protection for fundamental rights of individuals 'the fabric of international society will be built on precarious foundations'.[54] Despite the very few references that the UN Charter made to the protection of fundamental rights, it marked an important turning point that initiated a period where human rights would become a central topic for international law. The transformation of the protection of fundamental rights from a purely domestic issue into an international law affair was clearly settled when the UN Commission on Human Rights was established and tasked with the creation of a human rights document. The adoption of the Universal Declaration of Human Rights (UDHR) in 1948 by the General Assembly became a decisive moment that proclaimed the ever-continuing relationship between human rights and international law.[55]

2.2 *International Law as a Fertile Land*

The anchoring the human rights expansionist discourse into the framework of international law seems to have been deemed a very efficient discursive move. Fundamental rights were already part of domestic law of several states before 1945. Individuals were protected to a certain degree against the power of their government. Nevertheless, this was deemed to be insufficient. The legal

---

53 Recent accounts that inquire how human rights acquired its contemporary status have challenged this history that is told from a linear perspective. Moyn argued that the birth of human rights as the last utopia to elevate the human condition can be traced back to the 1970s. It is only after all other political projects and ideologies have failed that human rights emerged as the project that could protect the most basic norms. See Moyn, *The Last Utopia: Human Rights in History* (n 1).

54 Hersch Lauterpacht, *An International Bill of Rights of Man* (Oxford University Press, first ed. 1945, 2013), 7.

55 On the history of the Universal Declaration of Human Rights, see Mary Ann Glendon, *A World Made New: Eleanor Roosevelt and the Universal Declaration of Human Rights* (Random House 2002), Johannes Morsink, *The Universal Declaration of Human Rights: Origins, Drafting and Intent* (University of Pennsylvania Press 1999).

discourse came to be permeated by attempts to transform this national protection into an international one and establish a system where everyone around the globe would share similar fundamental rights. In other words, the transformation of the protection of fundamental rights from a mere domestic law issue into a matter that should be governed by international law is a deliberate choice of its architects. The adoption of the UDHR marked a pivotal moment that initiated the 'dual positivisation' of fundamental rights in domestic and international law.[56] While fundamental rights started to be protected at the domestic level before acquiring legal protection at the international level, nowadays the two legal orders are in constant dynamic interplay.[57] The primary purpose of both domestic and international protection of fundamental rights is to limit the power of sovereign against arbitrary action.[58] It can be questioned, however, why the legal protection provided at the domestic level was insufficient and human rights were also transposed into international law.

Why did international law come to be a better discursive route for the development of human rights? It should be emphasised that this question is different than asking what positive impact the development of international human rights law might have had on the protection of fundamental rights generally. It can be stated that dual positivisation has enforced the protection of fundamental rights by providing a legal framework that guarantees the rights of not only citizens but also non-citizens of a state, ensuring the extra-territorial application of international human rights treaties or creating positive obligations for states.[59] These are, however, outcomes of developing an international legal framework for the protection of individuals' interests and not particularly reasons for why at the first place there was a need for the internationalisation of this protection.

Many reasons can be listed why international law provided a favourable space for human rights to flourish and consolidate. First, universality of international law is an important aspect that was deemed to be highly beneficial for the human rights expansionist discourse. International law is said

56 Gerald L Neuman, 'Human Rights and Constitutional Rights: Harmony and Dissonance', (2002) 55 Stanford Law Review 1863.

57 Samantha Besson, 'Human Rights and Constitutional Rights: Patterns of Mutual Validation and Legitimation' in Rowan Cruft, S Matthew Liao, and Massimo Renzo (eds.), *Philosophical Foundations of Human Rights* (Oxford University Press 2015) 279. Buchanan argued that this interplay further helps the two orders to legitimise one another, see Allen Buchanan, 'Reciprocal Legitimation: Reframing the Problem of International Legitimacy', (2011) 10 Politics, Philosophy & Economics 5–19.

58 Stephen Gardbaum, 'Human Rights as International Constitutional Rights', (2008) 19 European Journal of International Law 750.

59 Ibid 764–5.

to be universal. From a geographical perspective, this implies the application of international law globally in an equal manner to every international law actor. This understanding of universality which refers to its spatial outreach is a useful tool to justify the expansionist nature of human rights law. From a more substantive perspective, universality of international can be used to refer to the functionality of the field to create a harmonious and inclusive legal order. In that sense, the discourse on the universality of international law, both from a spatial or substantive perspective can help to disregard any difference in terms of power, legal history, political history, culture, language, religion in order to unite around the same legal order. This provides a fertile ground for human rights to declare and advance its universalist discursivity.[60] If human rights are rights that everyone should enjoy just by virtue of their humanity, rights need to be universal and applied to everyone equally.[61] The transformation of human rights into a topic that should be governed by international law is an endeavour that benefits extensively from the universalist discourse of international law.[62]

Second, the rich area of manoeuvre provided by the sources of international law can be put forward as another reason why the transposition of the protection of fundamental rights from domestic into international arena was deemed to be necessary. Sources of international law enable a large space of freedom for a discursive play which can easily accommodate the expansionist propensity of human rights law. In domestic legal orders, legislative power is often confined to an entity that is entitled to pass legislation that will be binding on everyone. Domestic legal protection of human rights will be limited to formal sources as they are regulated by the legislative. The decentralised structure of international law allows for the protection of human rights not only through international treaties but also customary international law and general principles of law that are open to extensive discursive innovations. The flexible structure of sources of international law provides the necessary space for the expansionist manoeuvres at work in the human rights discourse. It can be argued that anything that cannot be ascertained through international law

---

60 Samantha Besson, 'Human Rights and Constitutional Rights: Patterns of Mutual Validation and Legitimation' in Cruft, Liao, and Renzo (eds.), *Philosophical Foundations of Human Rights* (Oxford University Press 2015) 284.

61 Samantha Besson, 'The Egalitarian Dimension of Human Rights' in Archiv für Rechts- und Sozialphilosophie, ARSP. Beiheft, 2013, 136, 33, available at: https://hal.archives-ouvertes.fr/hal-02516267/document.

62 On the cultural specific scope of human rights as stemming from a European legal history and therefore inability to embody universality, see Makau Mutua, 'The Ideology of Human Rights', (1996) 36 Virginia Journal of International Law 589–658.

treaties can be captured through a customary rule or general principle of law.[63] The absence of a settled doctrine of customary international law[64] becomes a very attractive discursive terrain in terms of expansionism.[65] In that sense, customary international law provides the necessary discursive tools to discover new rules of human rights.[66] When international customary law cannot come to the rescue of the expansionist discursivity, general principles of law become another popular tool to stretch the limits of human rights law. Several scholars have already examined the essential role that general principles of law can play in expanding the scope of human rights.[67] They are not only used by international courts and human rights bodies to fill the gaps of international treaties and custom but rather, they can be instrumentalised to create new norms as well.[68]

Third, domesticating fundamental rights and turning them into a topic regulated by international law enhances the enforcement mechanisms of

63 Martti Koskenniemi, 'The Pull of the Mainstream', (1990) 88 Michigan Law Review 1947–8, Bruno Simma and Philip Alston, 'The Sources of Human Rights Law: Custom, Jus Cogens, and General Principles', (1988) 12 Australian Yearbook of International Law 83.

64 d'Aspremont, *Formalism and the Sources of International Law: A Theory of the Ascertainment of Legal Rules* (n 4) 162–170.

65 Koskenniemi, 'The Pull of the Mainstream', (n 63) 83.

66 Jean d'Aspremont, *The Discourse on Customary International Law* (Oxford University Press 2021).

67 Simma and Alston, 'The Sources of Human Rights Law: Custom, Jus Cogens, and General Principles', (n 63), Theodor Meron, *Human Rights and Humanitarian Norms as Customary Law* (Oxford University Press 1989), Hurst Hannum, 'The Status of the Universal Declaration of Human Rights in National and International Law', (1995) 25 Georgia Journal of International and Comparative Law 287, Jan Wouters and Cedric Ryngaert, 'Impact on the Process of the Formation of Customary International Law' in Kamminga and Scheinin (eds.), *The Impact of Human Rights Law on General International Law* (Oxford University Press 2009), William Felice 'The Right to Development' in David P Forsythe (ed.), *Encyclopedia of Human Rights* (Oxford University Press 2009). International courts have not been so generous in making use of general principles of law, see Allain Pellet and Daniel Müller, 'Article 38' in Andreas Zimmermann et al. (eds.), *The Statute of the International Court of Justice: A Commentary* (Oxford University Press 2019), Gleider Hernández, *The International Court of Justice and the Judicial Function* (Oxford University Press 2014) 261. The role of general principles of law in the ascertainment of rules might be changing with ILC adding the topic to its programme, see the Second Report of the Special Rapporteur, ILC, 'Second Report on General Principles of Law by Marcelo Vázquez-Bermúdez, Special Rapporteur', Geneva, 27 April–5 June and 6 July–7 August 2020, UN Doc A/CN.4/741. See also Imogen Saunders, *General Principles as a Source of International Law: Art 38 (1)(C) of the Statute of the International Court of Justice* (Bloomsbury Publishing 2021).

68 Robert Kolb, 'Principles as Sources of International Law (with Special Reference to Good Faith)', (2006) 53 Netherlands International Law Review 1–36.

these rights. Protection of fundamental rights at the domestic level is bound to follow the steps set out by the domestic legislation. When international courts and bodies are established to provide a supranational layer of protection, this undoubtedly contributes to the more effective enforcement of these rights.[69] Domestic and international monitoring mechanisms can also be said to complement one another.[70] When the Council of Europe drafted the European Convention on Human Rights, one of the primary aims was to establish an international court that would adjudicate on matters arising from the Convention.[71] In other words, the aim with the drafting of the ECHR was not only to provide a list of fundamental rights that should be recognised in member states of the Council of Europe but also to establish a human rights court that would provide an international remedy for violations of the Convention. Institutional authority of international law was in that sense deemed to be necessary for the effective implementation of human rights. Further, the international monitoring body whether it is a court, or a body set up by an international organisation, can find more liberty in its interpretation of that particular right in comparison to the national judge within the domestic framework. Progressive interpretation of international human rights can find a more fertile ground before international courts and international bodies.[72]

Another important aspect of the internationalisation of human rights protection is that it allows states to question how other states are treating their nationals.[73] As the textbook narrative goes, the domestic developments in the UK and the revolutionary movements in particular in France and the US have been highly influential in the drafting process of the Universal Declaration of Human Rights. When human rights law was taking shape in the early years of the UN, Western states had a considerable weight in the preparation of the human rights discursivity. The discourse of human rights was built on

69 Gardbaum, 'Human Rights as International Constitutional Rights', (n 58) 766.

70 Samantha Besson, 'Sources of International Human Rights Law: How General is General International Law' in Samantha Besson and Jean d'Aspremont (eds.), *The Oxford Handbook of the Sources of International Law* (Oxford University Press 2017) 859. On the subsidiarity of international human rights adjudication, see Robert Spano, 'Universality or Diversity of Human Rights? Strasbourg in the Age of Subsidiarity', (2014) 14 Human Rights Law Review 487–502, Gerald Neuman, 'Subsidiarity' in Shelton (ed.), *The Oxford Handbook of International Human Rights Law* (Oxford University Press 2013) 360.

71 Steven Greer, 'Europe' in Moeckli et al. (eds.), *International Human Rights Law* (Oxford University Press 2022) 447.

72 For some critical remarks on the favourable representations of international institutions in the international legal discourse, see Jean d'Aspremont, 'The Love for International Organizations', (2023) 20 International Organizations Law Review 111–159.

73 Gardbaum, 'Human Rights as International Constitutional Rights', (n 58) 766.

opposing the good against the evil which was an intentional structure of its Western architects.[74] The establishment of UN bodies for the monitoring of human rights and the establishment of regional human rights courts provided suitable tools for the imperialist policies of Western states. Inter-state complaint procedure allowed Western states to have a say about the treatment of individuals in other states. International monitoring could be instrumentalised to export the Western idea of what human rights should be and how they should be interpreted and implemented.[75] In that sense, the transposition of the protection of human rights from the domestic to the international sphere helped to create a new battlefield for the 'civilising mission'.[76]

The positivisation of fundamental rights in international law is essential, as it is in domestic law, to replace the language of morals with law. The relationship between morals and human rights has been extensively examined in the literature. Some scholars claim that legal human rights are mirroring a set of moral values.[77] For Griffin, moral human rights protect normative agency and rights that do not represent a moral value should not be codified in international legal instruments.[78] Buchanan was of the contrary view and argued that international human rights are not 'moral human rights in legal dress'.[79] He rather claimed that international human rights law establishes a system whereby states are legally required to respect certain universal standards for the benefit of individuals within their jurisdiction.[80] He opined that although during its inception human rights law relied on the consent of states, we might be moving towards an era where we will no longer require this consent in order to force states to abide by these minimal standards.[81] Besson argued that human rights are moral rights that are of such an importance that they have

74 Makau Mutua, 'Savages, Victims, and Saviors: The Metaphor of Human Rights', (2001) 42 Harvard International Law Journal 202.

75 Koskenniemi, 'The Pull of the Mainstream', (n 63).

76 Anthony Anghie, 'International Human Rights Law and a Developing World Perspective' in Sheeran and Rodley (eds.), *Routledge Handbook of International Human Rights Law* (Routledge 2016) 112.

77 Joseph Raz, 'Human Rights without Foundations' in Besson and Tasioulas (eds.), *The Philosophy of International Law* (Oxford University Press 2010) 321, James Griffin, *On Human Rights* (Oxford University Press 2009), Morsink, *The Universal Declaration of Human Rights: Origins, Drafting and Intent* (n 55).

78 Griffin, *On Human Rights* (n 77).

79 Buchanan, *The Heart of Human Rights* (n 36) 19.

80 Ibid 27.

81 Ibid 28.

been codified as legal rights.[82] According to Besson, not every moral interest would generate duties but it is only if a moral interest attains a certain threshold of importance they will be protected through law. She further claimed that not all human rights will necessarily correspond to a moral right.[83]

While the discussion between morals and human rights is a long debate that does not need to be further detailed here, the positivisation of human rights is an essential step in the transformation of these moral values into a matter governed by law. In the liberal legal order, law is expected to constitute a technical tool which provides objective and value neutral rules.[84] In this liberal order, legal rules serve their own interests and are emancipated from any other ultimate moral purpose.[85] This assumption that law is capable to be free from moral values and provides a technical tool relies on the belief that it provides itself with its own foundations.[86] This is especially of a particular importance in the case of human rights where there is a close kinship between the legal entitlements and the moral interests that they might reflect. When the interests inherent in moral rights are turned into legal rights and made part of the international legal framework, this allows to speak the language of law and it eliminates the necessity to justify why these interests should be protected from a moral perspective.[87] International law allows to decouple human rights from moral interests they might represent and turn them into legal entitlements that are guaranteed, implemented and protected through binding legal instruments. Regardless of the debate whether human rights mirror moral values or represent universal minimal standards, when they are made part of international law, they no longer constitute a catalogue of moral values that are good and should be followed but they are legal interests that benefit from the authority of international law. This allows human rights to distance itself from morality or politics and equips it with the ability to speak the language of rules and principles.

---

82 Samantha Besson, 'Sources of International Human Rights Law: How General is General International Law' in Besson and d'Aspremont (eds.), *The Oxford Handbook of the Sources of International Law* (Oxford University Press 2017) 837.

83 Ibid.

84 Koskenniemi, *From Apology to Utopia: The Structure of International Legal Argument* (n 40) 71–2.

85 Martti Koskenniemi, 'The Politics of International Law', (1990) 1 European Journal of International Law 4, Roberto Mangabeira Unger, *Knowledge and Politics* (Free Press 1976) 76–81.

86 Jean d'Aspremont, *International Law as a Belief System* (Cambridge University Press 2017) 11.

87 Buchanan, *The Heart of Human Rights* (n 36) 9.

An additional virtue of the positivisation of human rights in international law is that it brought about the mainstreaming of human rights since it reinforced the 'academic or diplomatic prestige' of the subject-matter.[88] Right after its establishment, the UN has become the beacon for the production, promotion and dissemination of human rights norms which allowed not only the participation of high-ranking state officials to the relevant debates but also it raised the profile of the human rights discourse by keeping it on the agenda. The human rights discourse gained a remarkable acceleration in the 1970s to dominate any debate about human dignity and justice to replace all other political ideologies that failed until that time.[89] It can be noted that not only human rights became mainstream by gaining a status in the international arena but further it established its prerogatives by setting up its own agenda.[90] As a special regime, human rights law managed to create new objectives that were mainly targeted towards the protection of the individual in a way that was not known to international law until the second half of the 20th century. Said differently, when human rights law became part of international law, this allowed to frame a certain problem as a human rights problem and provide solutions that would particularly meet the demands of this specific regime.[91] International human rights law created its own vocabulary to define new problems and solve them with its own rules and institutions.

2.3 *Crossing Discursive Borders*

Dual positivisation of fundamental rights at the domestic and international law was carried out simultaneously. While on one hand, fundamental rights were gaining more ground in constitutional instruments, the UN and several other regional organisations contributed to the development of human rights at the international level. As indicated in the previous section, anchoring the protection of fundamental rights into an international law framework came with various discursive advantages. However, this was not deemed to be enough. More could be accomplished to expand the sources of human rights law by stretching the limits of international law. Human rights law, after all, had very different objectives than international law. Some of the basic tenets of international law were not suitable to reach the objectives of human rights.

88 Koskenniemi, 'The Pull of the Mainstream', (n 63) 1962.

89 Moyn, *The Last Utopia: Human Rights in History* (n 1).

90 Martti Koskenniemi, 'The Fate of Public International Law: Between Technique and Politics', (2007) 70 The Modern Law Review 5.

91 Ibid 5–8.

Once again, a lot of discursive innovation came to be fuelled by the idea the the human rights discourse required a departure from general international law. Some principles of international law had to be either tailored or limited in order to achieve the objectives of the human rights agenda. In other words, there was an inevitable necessity to differentiate human rights law from general international law.

Several justifications can be put forward to claim that human rights law depart from general international law. The first claim relates to state 'sovereignty'. Sovereignty is a word that is used – rather sloppily – as a shorthand for many different things in the international legal discourse and whose actual meaning has remained very much in limbo.[92] Yet, in the discourse on international human rights law, sovereignty is usually mobilised as an obstructive concept that stands in opposition to human rights. If sovereignty is understood as the freedom of the state not to be compelled to act in a certain way without its consent, human rights create obligations that limit this freedom.[93] The relationship between human rights and sovereignty is often construed as a story of conflicting ends. From a traditional perspective international law is said to create an order between states to regulate their relations and it stays away from anything that can be considered within a state's domestic affairs. The way states treated their nationals was a matter that was left to the discretion of states for a long time. Sovereignty, in this regard, provided states with the power to assert that no state could intervene in their internal affairs to dictate how individuals should be treated. The elaboration of the human rights expansionist discourse as part of general international law is positioned against this understanding of sovereignty. International human rights law aimed at limiting the sovereignty

92 It could be argued that international lawyers' sovereignty is a non-sovereign sovereignty for it tolerates limitation. See Jean d'Aspremont, *After Meaning: The Sovereignty of Forms in International Law* (Edward Elgar 2021) viii. On the idea that divisible sovereignty is no longer sovereignty as it would otherwise not be sovereign, see Jacques Derrida, *The Beast and the Sovereign*, vol 1 (University of Chicago Press 2011) 57, 76–77. See also Jacques Derrida, *Papier Machine* (Galilée 2001) 345.

93 Hélène Ruiz Fabri, 'Sovereignty and Human Rights' in Philip Alston and Euan Macdonald (eds.), *Human Rights, Intervention, and the Use of Force* (Oxford University Press 2008) 38. For an account that does not treat human rights and sovereignty in opposition to one another, see Christian Reus-Smit, 'Human Rights and the Social Construction of Sovereignty', (2001) 27 Review of International Studies 519–38. For a critique of the opposition between sovereignty and human rights from a Third World Approach, see BS Chimni, 'Sovereignty, Rights, and Armed Intervention: A Dialectical Perspective' in Hilary Charlesworth and Jean-Marc Coicaud (eds.), *Fault Lines of International Legitimacy* (Cambridge University Press 2010) 303.

of states by determining some minimal standards that states should adopt in their domestic legal framework. Contrary to the traditional understanding where states enjoyed the liberty to regulate their internal affairs, the human rights expansionist discourse can be seen as an endeavour that aimed to confine state sovereignty into stricter limits.[94]

The aim of the human rights expansionist discourse can be construed as being at odds with one of the basic tenets of general international law which requires international actors not to intervene in one another's domestic jurisdiction. In other words, the development of international human rights law has become a useful tool for those who aspired to redefine what sovereignty means in international law.[95] Following the development of the human rights expansionist discourse, the protection of individuals ceased to be a matter that is essentially within the domestic jurisdiction of a state. The atrocities of the Second World War have played an essential role in objecting to the understanding that it is outside the purview of international law to dictate states how they should treat their citizens.[96] In that sense, what was once regarded as objects and subjects of domestic law have started to carve out a role in international law.[97] The UN Charter can be considered a turning point in the way the contours of state sovereignty are determined by including human rights in the agenda of international law. This was followed by the adoption of the Universal Declaration of Human Rights which has become the first international law instrument to include a set of fundamental rights. It should be noted that limitations on what is commonly called 'sovereignty' did not start in international law with the development of human rights law. The innovative aspect of human rights is that it allegedly limits sovereignty for the sake of individuals in the domestic jurisdiction of the state.[98] While some interpreted the changing nature of state sovereignty as a shift of focus from state values to human

94 Frédéric Mégret, 'International Human Rights Law Theory' in Alexander Orakhelashvili (ed.), *Research Handbook on the Theory and History of International Law* (Edward Elgar Publishing 2020) 177.

95 W Michael Reisman, 'Sovereignty and Human Rights in Contemporary International Law', (1990) 84 *American Journal of International Law* 872.

96 Louis Henkin, 'That S Word: Sovereignty, and Globalization, and Human Rights, Et Cetera', (1999) 68 Fordham Law Review 4.

97 Samantha Besson, 'The Authority of International Law: Lifting the State Veil', (2009) 31 Sydney Law Review 349.

98 Buchanan, *The Heart of Human Rights* (n 36) 23.

values,[99] others explained it as a shift from national sovereignty to popular sovereignty.[100]

The second claim about the dissonance between principles of international law and the objectives of human rights law relates to the principle of voluntarism which dictates that states can only be bound with obligations to which they give their consent.[101] It was claimed that this principle could not easily be reconciled with the demands of human rights law.[102] At its very centre, human rights embody the idea that states accept certain minimal standards of conduct for those who live within their jurisdiction. In the 1940s when the human rights expansionist discourse was emerging, the mainstream perspective viewed international law as emanating from the free will of states.[103] This traditional understanding of international legal positivism was premised on the idea that states could be bound only with obligations to which they have given their consent. The human rights discourse witnessed a strong reliance on the special character of human rights obligations to stretch the limits of voluntarism in international law. Since the primary purpose of human rights is to protect the interest of the individual against the state, this has provided a solid ground to attach little importance to the principle of voluntarism. Christakis, for instance, identified several areas including the diminishing role of *travaux préparatoires* in the interpretation of international human rights treaties, the extensive use of soft law, the creation of 'positive obligations', the use of jus cogens as a trump, judicial activism, where the traditional principle of voluntarism came to take a back seat in the legal discourse.[104] It can even be argued that international human rights law epitomises the anti-consensualist posture in the current international legal order.[105]

99 Louis Henkin, 'Human Rights and State Sovereignty', (1995) 25 *Georgia Journal of International and Comparative Law* 35.

100 Besson, 'The Authority of International Law: Lifting the State Veil', (n 97) 374.

101 For some critical view on the very idea of consent to international law, see Jean d'Aspremont, 'Consenting to International Law in Five Moves' in Samantha Besson (ed.), Consenting to International Law (Cambridge University Press 2023) 117–134.

102 Henkin, 'Human Rights and State Sovereignty', (n 99), Allen Buchanan, *Justice, Legitimacy, and Self-Determination: Moral Foundations for International Law* (Oxford University Press 2007), Thomas Pogge, *Realizing Rawls* (Cornell University Press 1989).

103 S.S. 'Lotus' (France v. Turkey), Judgment of 7 September 1927, PCIJ Series A No. 10 (1927) 18.

104 For a traditional view on this question, see Théodore Christakis, 'Human Rights from a Neo-Voluntarist Perspective' in Jörg Kammerhofer and Jean d'Aspremont (eds.), *International Legal Positivism in a Post-Modern World* (Cambridge University Press 2014) 425–37.

105 Ibid 424.

The third claim relates to the different actors of the two fields and in particular the emergence of the individual as an actor in international law. International law is said to regulate relations between states, while human rights law protects individuals against arbitrary actions of states. One of the most remarkable developments in 20th century international law has been the rise of the non-state actor.[106] While international law was mostly concerned with relations between states up until the 20th century with some exceptions, this has started to change with the establishment of international organisations[107] and especially the new role of the individual in the international arena.[108] Traditional international law does not concern itself with individuals which were long regarded as mere objects who did not possess any leverage against their state.[109] It is only with the progress of human rights law that individuals started to have a say in international law and be considered an actor of the field alongside states and international organisations.[110] In that sense, international law has been designed to regulate relations between states which are equal to one another in a horizontal system. Whereas, in human rights law individuals can claim their rights from the state while still maintaining a vertical relationship in domestic law. The design of international law when it comes to the actors and their relations with one another had to be tailored in line with the demands of human rights.

The above-mentioned claims provide fertile ground to pull away human rights law from general international law to bestow the former with a special

106 Reparation for Injuries Suffered in the Service of the United Nations, Advisory Opinion, ICJ Reports 1949, 174, 178–9.

107 David Kennedy, 'The Move to Institutions', (1987) 8 Cardozo Law Review 841–988, Jan Klabbers, 'The EJIL Foreword: The Transformation of International Organizations Law', (2015) 26 *European Journal of International Law* 9–82.

108 Steve Charnovitz, 'Nongovernmental Organizations and International Law', (2006) 100 American Journal of International Law 348–72.

109 Lassa Oppenheim, *International Law: A Treatise, Volume I* (Longmans 2018) 341.

110 Hersch Lauterpacht, *International Law and Human Rights* (Stevens 1950) 72, Anne Peters, *Beyond Human Rights: The Legal Status of the Individual in International Law* (Cambridge University Press 2016) 11–34, Robert McCorquodale, 'The Individual and the International Legal System' in Malcolm Evans (ed.), *International Law* (Oxford University Press 2018), Andrew Clapham, 'The Role of the Individual in International Law', (2010) 21 European Journal of International Law 25–30, Rosalyn Higgins, 'Conceptual Thinking About the Individual in International Law', (1978) 4 British Journal of International Studies 1–19, Alexander Orakhelashvili, 'The Position of the Individual in International Law', (2000) 31 California Western International Law Journal 241, Kate Parlett, *The Individual in the International Legal System: Continuity and Change in International Law* (Cambridge University Press 2011).

character. These three claims form the foundation for the argument that the nature of human rights obligations differ from the obligations of general international law. It is on this basis that the legal discourse came to be the site of creative moves and constructions meant to detach human rights from general international law. The argument that the objectives of human rights law do not reconcile with these principles of international law became a first step for further discursive moves that allowed to expand the scope of human rights. The deadlock created with the principles of international law and the demands of human rights can be resolved, however, by bestowing a special character to the obligations created by human rights. When human rights are pulled away from general international law by relying on the 'special character' of its obligations, this allows to deny the application of general international law rules that do not accommodate with the purpose of human rights. The first block that needs to be built in order to claim that human rights law is a special regime is to demonstrate that the nature of obligations is different from the nature of obligations in general international law. In general international law, treaties establish reciprocal obligations between the signatory states. When states become parties to human rights treaties, however, they undertake these obligations towards those living under their jurisdiction, rather than the other signatories. This non-reciprocal character of human rights obligations allowed the human rights discourse to differentiate itself from general international law. After it is demonstrated that the nature of obligations in these two fields cannot be reconciled, this is followed by a differentiation in specific subjects including reservations, succession, limitation of obligations, withdrawal etc. The following chapter turns to these discursive moves that have been witnessed in the legal discourse for the sake of expanding human rights law.

3 Oscillation between Generalism and Exceptionalism

It is often contended that due to some of its peculiar characteristics the discursive tools of general international law cannot be directly applied to human rights law. In other words, it is claimed that the discursive tools in general international law are not adequate to be applied to human rights law. The discursive constructions of international law need to be tailored to these specific characteristics of human rights law. These exceptionalist claims whereby human rights law is differentiated from international law provide ample ground to interpret human rights in such a way that it helps broadening its scope. The exceptionalist claims are often followed by generalist claims that underline that human rights are nevertheless anchored into general international law and can benefit from the discursive constructions of the latter. As is argued here, it is this constant oscillation between exceptionalist and generalist claims that supports and organises the expansionism of international human rights law.

This exceptionalism relies on the idea that general international law is made up of different self-contained regimes which all have their different discursive moves. As discussed previously, this is often labelled as the fragmentation of international law whereby different normative systems co-exist at an equal level as part of international law.[111] Fragmentation of international law can be opposed to the reconciliation approach whereby the two sperate regimes of human rights and international law are to be reconciled.[112] This study takes a different approach by focusing on the discursive blossoming that came to be witnessed in the legal discourse for the sake of expansionism. This chapter traces the generalist claims that have been put forward to confirm the commitment of the human rights expansionist discourse to general international law (3.1.) and the exceptionalist claims whereby human rights are pulled away from general international law (3.2.).

3.1 *Generalism at Play*

While international human rights law tries to build its own discursive moves in order to broaden its scope, this does not mean that it wants a total emancipation from the rules governing general international law. Since its inception, there has been no debate that international human rights law benefit from some of the same rules that are applicable in general international law. For instance, the entry into force of international human rights treaties or general principles governing international treaty law have been applied to this specific regime without much debate. The endeavour to pull away human rights law

111 See supra section 1.3. See also, International Law Commission, Report of the Working Group on Long-term Programme of Work, Risks Ensuing from the Fragmentation of International Law, ILC (LII)/WG/LT/L.1/Add.1 (25 July 2000), 25–43. See also, Koskenniemi and Leino, 'Fragmentation of International Law? Postmodern Anxieties', (n 25), Prost, *The Concept of Unity in Public International Law* (n 21), Sahib Singh, 'The Potential of International Law: Fragmentation and Ethics', (2011) 24 Leiden Journal of International Law 23–43.

112 Kamminga, 'Final Report on the Impact of International Human Rights Law on General International Law' in Menno Kamminga and Martin Scheinin (eds.), *The Impact of Human Rights Law on General International Law* (Oxford University Press 2009). International Law Association's 2008 Report on the impact of international human rights law on general international law states that the reconciliation approach is more in line with international practice and should be adopted.

from general international law by emphasising the different nature of these obligations is balanced out by an exercise to show that human rights is still solidly anchored in general international law. While the legal discourse show a strong tendency to subject human rights law to different discursive innovations, this move away from international law eventually does not go as far as creating a total rupture.

The ILC's report on the fragmentation of international law noted that it is important for special regimes to preserve their connection with general international law. The report stated that whenever special regimes do not suffice to provide a solution, it is necessary to return back to general international law and make use of its general rules and principles to fill any possible gap.[113] This is also one of the reasons why the ILC Report refers to different normative orders that co-exist in international legal order as 'special regime' rather than 'self-contained regime' since these normative orders are never totally self-contained.[114] Special regimes necessarily have to rely on general international law when the different discursive moves created for the particular purposes and needs of that regime are not sufficient or do not provide the desired outcome. This inevitable oscillation between the special regime and general international law serves an important mission to ensure the unity of international law as well. When the special regimes are not self-contained independent orders from general international law, it helps to consider international law as a system where any contradiction can be eradicated by this constant oscillation between special regimes and general international law.[115]

The necessity for special regimes to fall back on general international law was also implied by the ICJ in the case of Nicaragua.[116] The Court seems to have indicated that whenever a special regime provides a certain form of remedy for a violation of an obligation, that should take precedence over remedies provided by general international law. The Court stated that:

113 Fragmentation of International Law: Difficulties Arising from the Diversification and Expansion of International', Report of the Study Group of the International Law Commission, Finalized by Martti Koskenniemi, UN Doc A/CN.4/L.682 (13 April 2006), para. 192.

114 Ibid para. 193. In the same line, see Bruno Simma, 'Self-Contained Regimes', (1985) 16 Netherlands Yearbook of International Law 111–36, Bruno Simma and Dirk Pulkowski, 'Of Planets and the Universe: Self-Contained Regimes in International Law', (2006) 17 European Journal of International Law 483–529.

115 Koskenniemi, 'The Fate of Public International Law: Between Technique and Politics', (n 90) 17.

116 Simma and Pulkowski, 'Of Planets and the Universe: Self-Contained Regimes in International Law', (n 114) 524–5.

> where human rights are protected by international conventions, that protection takes the form of such arrangements for monitoring or ensuring respect for human rights as are provided for in the conventions themselves ... The Court has noted above (paragraph 168) that the Nicaraguan Government has since 1979 ratified a number of international instruments on human rights, and one of these was the American Convention on Human Rights (the Pact of San José, Costa Rica). The mechanisms provided for therein have functioned.[117]

The Court further noted because the mechanisms established by regional human rights treaties have been effective, there was no need to resort to remedies provided by general international law. Simma and Pulkowski argued that it was clear indication by the Court that it is only if the remedies provided by the regional human rights treaties were to be ineffective that it would be possible to make use of mechanisms provided by general international law.[118]

The following sections discuss how the creation of new discursive moves for human rights law does not go as far as breaking the connection with general international law. The reliance on inter-state applications for human rights violations and the establishment of institutional processes for their remedies is an important move to anchor human rights into the framework of general international law. It is also significant that the Vienna Convention on the Law of Treaties plays an essential role in human rights law especially regarding interpretation of treaties.

3.1.1 Inter-State Applications

The basis of the claim that international human rights law differs from general international law relies on the special character of human rights obligations. As it will be explained below, because human rights protect the interests of individuals, they are given the power to bring a claim against their state before international bodies and courts when they allege the violation of a human rights treaty. This does not rule out the right of a state to bring a claim against another state in case of a violation. This is exemplified by the possibility that several international human rights treaties provide for inter-state applications that can be made for the non-performance of the treaty. Indeed, the ICCPR,[119]

117 Military and Paramilitary Activities in and against Nicaragua (Nicaragua v United States), Merits, ICJ Reports 1986, para. 267.

118 Simma and Pulkowski, 'Of Planets and the Universe: Self-Contained Regimes in International Law', (n 114) 524–5.

119 Article 41: 'A State Party to the present Covenant may at any time declare under this article that it recognizes the competence of the Committee to receive and consider

ECHR,[120] ACHR,[121] ACHPR[122] allow inter-state applications. This shows that human rights treaties are not solely adopted for states to protect fundamental rights of those who are within their jurisdiction, but the signatories are also provided with a right to bring a claim against a wrongdoing state. The recognition of inter-state applications before international bodies showcases how despite their special character, human rights obligations maintain their close relationship with general international law. This demonstrates the oscillation between an exceptionalist approach that emphasises the special character of human rights obligations and a generalist approach that still tries to anchor these obligations into a general international law framework. This is also exemplified by the General Comment 31 of the Human Rights Committee which reminds that every state has an interest in the performance of the ICCPR:

> While article 2 is couched in terms of the obligations of State Parties towards individuals as the right-holders under the Covenant, every State Party has a legal interest in the performance by every other State Party of its obligations … Furthermore, the contractual dimension of the treaty involves any State Party to a treaty being obligated to every other State Party to comply with its undertakings under the treaty. In this connection, the Committee reminds States Parties of the desirability of making the declaration contemplated in article 41.[123]

This statement by the Human Rights Committee underlines that it is not only individuals who should enjoy the rights enshrined the ICCPR but that every state does have an interest for all signatories to put these rights into practice.

---

communications to the effect that a State Party claims that another State Party is not fulfilling its obligations under the present Covenant.' in International Covenant on Civil and Political Rights, 16 December 1966, 999 UNTS 171 (entered into force 23 March 1976).

120 Artice 33: 'Any High Contracting Party may refer to the Court any alleged breach of the provisions of the Convention and the Protocols thereto by another High Contracting Party.'

121 Article 45: 'Any State Party may, when it deposits its instrument of ratification of or adherence to this Convention, or at any later time, declare that it recognizes the competence of the Commission to receive and examine communications in which a State Party alleges that another State Party has committed a violation of a human right set forth in this Convention.'

122 Article 47: 'If a State Party to the present Charter has good reasons to believe that another State Party to this Charter has violated the provisions of the Charter, it may draw, by written communication, the attention of that State to the matter.'

123 UN Human Rights Committee, General Comment 31 (26 May 2004), UN Doc CCPR/C/21/Rev.1/Add. 13.

The Human Rights Committee further calls upon states to make a declaration under article 41 of the ICCPR which allows the Committee to receive and consider inter-state applications. The inclusion of inter-state applications in the ICCPR is a clear indication that while the main purpose of the treaty is to protect individuals, there is still some reciprocity in these obligations which allows inter-state claims. In that regard, the nature of human rights obligations is not strictly non-reciprocal but enjoys both reciprocity and non-reciprocity at the same time. This oscillation between exceptionalism of human rights obligations by relying on their non-reciprocal character and generalism that stems from their nevertheless reciprocal character provides ample ground to expand discursive innovations of international human rights law. This allows human rights to both benefit from the discursive moves available in general international law, such as inter-state applications, but also to make use of new discursive constructions by relying on the exceptional character of human rights obligations.[124]

3.1.2 The Vienna Convention on the Law of Treaties

International courts and bodies have not shied away from making use of the Vienna Convention on the Law of Treaties. The rules of interpretation as prescribed by the Vienna Convention have been frequently used by the Inter-American Court of Human Rights and UN human rights bodies.[125] This is also the case for the European Court of Human Rights that has relied on the rules of interpretation of the Vienna Convention in one of its earliest decisions.[126] The European Court ruled that the European Convention on Human Rights is an international treaty that creates obligations of an objective character that goes beyond reciprocal engagements between states.[127] While the ECtHR emphasised the special character of human rights obligations arising from the European Convention, it underlined how the Convention should be interpreted in line with the principles of interpretation prescribed by international law. The former president of the Court, Judge Costa, stated that the European Convention is to be interpreted in light of the Vienna Convention on the Law of Treaties.[128] In that sense, there is no question that the European Court follows the general rules of international law set by the Vienna Convention, in particular when it comes to rules of interpretation. This is further illustrated by the case-law of the Court. In the case of Bankovic, the

124 See infra 3.2.

125 Christakis, 'Human Rights from a Neo-Voluntarist Perspective' (n 104) 437.

126 Golder v UK (1975) ECtHR Ser A No 18, 1 EHRR 524, para. 213.

127 ECHR, Ireland v. UK (1978), 18 January 1978, Series A no. 25, para. 239.

128 Jean-Paul Costa, 'On the Legitimacy of the European Court of Human Rights' Judgments', (2011) 7 European Constitutional Law Review 176–7.

European Court of Human Rights stated in express terms how the Court is bound to implement the general rules of international law:

> The Court recalls that the Convention must be interpreted in the light of the rules set out in the Vienna Convention 1969 … It will, therefore, seek to ascertain the ordinary meaning to be given to the phrase "within their jurisdiction" in its context and in the light of the object and purpose of the Convention … Moreover, Article 31 § 3 (c) indicates that account is to be taken of "any relevant rules of international law applicable in the relations between the parties". More generally, the Court recalls that the principles underlying the Convention cannot be interpreted and applied in a vacuum. The Court must also take into account any relevant rules of international law when examining questions concerning its jurisdiction and, consequently, determine State responsibility in conformity with the governing principles of international law, although it must remain mindful of the Convention's special character as a human rights treaty.[129]

3.2 *Exceptionalism at Play*

While international human rights law anchors itself into general international law and benefits from its discursive moves, it systematically seeks to detach itself from it. It is in that context that new patterns of reasoning that move away human rights from general international law came to be witnessed in the legal discourse. It is only by discovering new discursive moves that would specifically apply to international human rights law that one can evidence why human rights law constitutes a special regime. The following sections examine these discursive moves that have been observed in the legal discourse and whose goal is to detach human rights from the rigid modes of discursivity of general international law.

3.2.1 The Nature of Obligations

The idea that the nature of obligations in human rights law is different from the nature of obligations in general international law plays an essential role in human rights exceptionalism. It is commonly argued that the nature of human rights law obligations differs from the nature of general international

129 Banković v Belgium et al App No 52207/99, ECHR 2001-XII, para. 55–57. Similarly, see Loizidou v Turkey (Preliminary Objections) (1995) 20 EHRR 99, para. 44, Al-Adsani v UK, ECHR No 35763/97, ECHR 2001-XI, 34 EHRR 11 (Grand Chamber), para. 40. On the application of general rules of international law in human rights cases, see generally, Campbell Mclachlan, 'The Principle of Systemic Integration and Article 31 (3)(C) of the Vienna Convention', (2005) 54 International & Comparative Law Quarterly 279–320.

law obligations.[130] While in general international law states owe obligations to one another, when they undertake human rights law obligations, they commit to respect these rights towards those who are within their jurisdiction, rather than other states. International human rights treaties can provide a unity between states as to what human rights obligations should entail and also help states to take a position with regard to their approach to human rights.[131] This difference between general international law and human rights treaties generates an essential argument to claim that the latter requires a different mode of reasoning. Indeed, this is a crucial rupture point between the two fields since the difference in nature of obligations has an overarching power to influence the applicability of several rules on treaty interpretation, reservations, succession to treaties, diplomatic protection etc. Once it has been established that human rights law obligations have a special and distinct character than general international law obligations, this provides a wide discursive space to allow the expansion – as it is understood here – of the scope and content of human rights.

This difference between the nature of human rights and general international law obligations is often explained by the non-reciprocity of obligations in human rights law.[132] A general international law treaty creates reciprocal obligations between states that accept to be bound by that treaty. In that sense, states owe these obligations to one another. On the other hand, human rights obligations are not reciprocal. When states accept to be bound by a human rights treaty, they do not owe these obligations to other states, but to persons within their jurisdiction. The beneficiaries of human rights treaties are not other signatories of the treaty but non-parties who are individuals.[133] A corollary of this difference is the non-contractual nature of human rights treaties.[134] States do not become a party to a human rights treaty in order to ensure that other states will respect these rights as well. They are rather committing themselves to protect certain minimal standards for those within their jurisdiction. This difference between the nature of obligations in human rights

130 Lea Brilmayer, 'From 'Contract' to 'Pledge': The Structure of International Human Rights Agreements', *Yale Law School, Faculty Scholarship Series, Paper 3753*, available at https://openyls.law.yale.edu/handle/20.500.13051/3174, (2006), Higgins, *Problems and Process: International Law and How We Use It* (n 14) 95–96.

131 Oona Hathaway, 'Do Human Rights Treaties Make a Difference' (2002) 111 Yale Journal of International Law 2005.

132 Dinah Shelton, *Remedies in International Human Rights Law* (Oxford University Press 2005) 97.

133 Brilmayer, 'From 'Contract' to 'Pledge': The Structure of International Human Rights Agreements', (n 14) 165.

134 Mégret, 'Nature of Obligations' (n 43) 89.

and international law is usually called the 'special character' of human rights obligations.

One of the earliest references to the special character of human rights obligations, albeit implicitly, was made by the International Court of Justice in its Advisory Opinion on the Genocide Convention. In 1950, the General Assembly of the UN asked the ICJ whether a reserving state could still be considered a party to a treaty if some states objected to its reservation. In its Advisory Opinion, the Court made some important statements regarding the nature of human rights obligations:

> The objects of such a convention must also be considered. The Convention was manifestly adopted for a purely humanitarian and civilizing purpose. It is indeed difficult to imagine a convention that might have this dual character to a greater degree, since its object on the one hand is to safeguard the very existence of certain human groups and on the other to confirm and endorse the most elementary principles of morality. In such a convention the contracting States do not have any interests of their own; they merely have, one and all, a common interest, namely, the accomplishment of those high purposes which are the *raison d'être* of the convention. Consequently, in a convention of this type one cannot speak of individual advantages or disadvantages to States, or of the maintenance of a perfect contractual balance between rights and duties. The high ideals which inspired the Convention provide, by virtue of the common will of the parties, the foundation and measure of all its provisions.[135]

Here, the ICJ underlined that the Genocide Convention did not create contractual obligations whereby states aimed at protecting their own interests. Contracting states committed to realise one common ideal which was the *raison d'être* of the Convention, namely the prevention of the crime of genocide.

The European Court of Human Rights made a similar statement in the case of Ireland v. UK by emphasising that the European Convention on Human Rights goes beyond establishing bilateral commitments: 'the Convention comprises more than reciprocal engagements between the contracting States. It creates, over and above a network of mutual, bilateral undertakings, objective obligations which, in the words of the Preamble, benefit from a "collective enforcement"'.[136] Similarly, the Human Rights Committee indicated in its

135 Reservations to the Genocide Convention (Advisory Opinion) [1951] ICJ Rep 15, para. 23.

136 ECHR, Ireland v. UK (1978), 18 January 1978, Series A no. 25, para. 239.

General Comment 24 that '[s]uch treaties, and the Covenant specifically, are not a web of inter-State exchanges of mutual obligations. They concern the endowment of individuals with rights.'[137]

The non-contractual character of human rights, in other words the special character of human rights obligations, constitutes the first step in human rights exceptionalism. It is under the banner of the special character of human rights obligations that new discursive moves emerged in the legal discourse and whose aim was to detach human rights law from general international law. The following sections that examine these various discursive innovations all rely on the contention that human rights obligations differ from general international law obligations by creating non-contractual commitments.

3.2.2 Breach of Obligations

When one establishes that human rights obligations have a special character and that they differ from general international law obligations due to their non-reciprocal character, this provides the foundation upon which many other exceptions can be built.

The way in which states can react to the non-fulfilment of obligations arising from general international law and human rights treaties varies considerably. As the primary source regulating treaty law, the Vienna Convention on the Law of Treaties provides specific rules on non-fulfilment of treaty obligations. Article 60 of the Vienna Convention regulates that in case there is a material breach other parties to the treaty can 'invoke the breach as a ground for terminating the treaty or suspending its operation in whole or in part'.[138] The article provides two alternatives in case a state does not respect their treaty obligations: signatory states can either suspend or terminate the treaty. In order to make recourse to article 60, there needs to be a material breach, which is according to paragraph 3, 'a repudiation of the treaty not sanctioned by the present Convention; or the violation of a provision essential to the accomplishment of the object or purpose of the treaty'. This is a corollary of the reciprocal character of international treaties whereby parties commit to undertake their obligations with the expectation that the other party will honour their obligations in return.[139] In the absence of compulsory dispute settlement, article 60

137 UN Human Rights Committee, General Comment 24 (11 November 1994), UN Doc CCPR/C/21/Rev.1/Add.6.

138 Article 60, Vienna Convention on the Law of Treaties (adopted 23 May 1969, entered into force 27 January 1980) 1155 UNTS 331.

139 Thomas Giegerich, 'Article 60' in Oliver Dörr and Kirsten Schmalenbach (eds.), *Vienna Convention on the Law of Treaties: A Commentary* (Springer 2018) 1096. This is reflected in Article 26 of the Vienna Convention with the principle of *pacta sunt servanda*, see

provides a form of self-help to the parties when there is a material breach of the treaty. It allows to recalibrate the balance of the contractual relationship that was damaged because of the party at fault.[140]

The non-performance of a human rights treaty, however, does not give other signatory states the right to suspend their obligations since their obligations are towards those within their jurisdiction, rather than other states.[141] The Vienna Convention is tailored to meet the special character of human rights treaties. Article 60/5 provides an important regulation regarding human rights exceptionalism and states that this form of self-help cannot be applied to provisions that aim to protect the human person. It states that '[p]aragraphs 1 to 3 do not apply to provisions relating to the protection of the human person contained in treaties of a humanitarian character, in particular to provisions prohibiting any form of reprisals against persons protected by such treaties.' This provides an exception to the general rule on suspension or termination of international law treaties of a general character in cases of non-performance. The provision was added to the Convention at the initiative of the Swiss delegation which argued that the Geneva Conventions, together with other human rights treaties, should not be subject to termination or suspension due to non-performance of a single state since they aim at protecting individuals rather than states' reciprocal interests.[142] This exception recognised only for treaties that protect the human person prohibits that human rights treaties are easily terminated or suspended due to a material breach. This ensures the stability of human rights treaties by excluding a form of self-help in case of a non-fulfilment of an obligation by one of the parties.[143] In its Advisory Opinion on Legal Consequences for States of the Continued Presence of South Africa in Namibia, the ICJ indicated that according to a general principle of law 'a right of termination on account of breach must be presumed to exist in respect of all treaties, except as regards provisions relating to the protection of the human person contained in treaties of a humanitarian character (as indicated in Art. 60, para. 5, of the Vienna Convention)'.[144] It is worth mentioning that this exceptional rule recognised for human rights treaties do comply with

---

Vienna Convention on the Law of Treaties (adopted 23 May 1969, entered into force 27 January 1980) 1155 UNTS 331.

140 Giegerich, 'Article 60' (n 139) 1097.

141 Brilmayer, 'From 'Contract' to 'Pledge': The Structure of International Human Rights Agreements', (n 14) 178.

142 Giegerich, 'Article 60' (n 139) 1020–21.

143 Christian Tams, 'Treaty Breaches and Responses' in Christian Tams and Antonios Tzanakopoulos (eds.), *Research Handbook on the Law of Treaties* (Edward Elgar 2014) 487.

144 Legal Consequences for States of the Continued Presence of South Africa in Namibia (South West Africa) notwithstanding Security Council Resolution 276 (1970), Advisory Opinion, ICJ Reports 1971, para. 96.

the preamble of the Convention which makes reference to 'universal respect for, and observance of, human rights and fundamental freedoms for all' in its 6th paragraph.

The wording of article 60/5 is broad enough to encompass any treaty that protects the human person, including both treaties that specifically deal with human rights and also humanitarian law treaties. The article requires two conditions: the provision should be about the protection of the person and enshrined in a treaty of a humanitarian character.[145] Here, the reciprocal character of general international law treaties is contrasted with the purpose of human rights treaties which is about the protection of the person. It can be argued that inter-state reciprocity is considered alien to the nature of human rights treaties.[146] Since general international law treaties protect reciprocal interests, if one party is in a material breach, the other party can take a unilateral action and decide to terminate or suspend the treaty. When it comes to international human rights treaties, since the purpose of the treaty is to protect fundamental rights, a unilateral action aiming to terminate or suspend the treaty would go against the purpose of the treaty. It would defeat the purpose of the treaty to allow other parties to terminate or suspend it due to the breach of a single state. In that sense, article 60/5 of the Vienna Convention provides an exceptional measure to accommodate the difference between the purposes of international law and human rights treaties and regulate different regimes for breach of obligations.

3.2.3 Standing

The rules on standing generate another source of differentiation between general international law and human rights law. Indeed, the argument that the nature of obligations in human rights law has a special character also bears upon the establishment of who has standing to make a claim when there is a violation. Traditionally, general international law creates bilateral obligations between states. This has two major consequences: it is the injured state that has standing to respond to the breach and invocation of responsibility of the state at fault is exclusive to the individually injured state.[147] It remains uncontroversial that the injured state has standing to invoke the responsibility of the

145 Giegerich, 'Article 60' (n 139) 1122.

146 Theodor Meron, *Human Rights Law-Making in the United Nations: A Critique of Instruments and Process* (Oxford University Press 1986) 146–147.

147 Christian Tams, *Enforcing Obligations Erga Omnes in International Law* (Cambridge University Press 2005) 48.

wrongful state, however the invocation of responsibility by states that are not directly injured by the breach has significantly changed with the emergence of the concept of *erga omnes*. Standing in general interest is a debate that dates back to earliest writings on international law.[148] However, the rising number of multilateral treaties in the 19th and 20th century brought about a greater concern regarding who would have standing when there is a breach of an obligation that does not create a direct injury to signatory states.

In general international law, in case there is a violation, the injured party has standing to make a claim. According to article 42 of International Law Commission's Articles on State Responsibility for Wrongful Acts (ARSIWA), an injured state can invoke the responsibility of another state if the obligation owed to that state is breached.[149] This rule establishes that the invocation of responsibility in international law primarily lies with the injured state. The Commentary states that the invocation of responsibility can take several forms which will usually be of a formal character such as initiating proceedings before international courts or resorting to countermeasures.[150] As stated in the Commentary of ARSIWA, article 42 is very closely related to article 60 of the VCLT. There are, however, two important differences. First, article 60 is concerned with violations which constitute a 'material breach' and can be applicable only regarding obligations arising from international treaties. As regards article 42 of the ARSIWA, the obligation can arise from treaties or other sources and the violation does not have to be a 'material breach' for the injured state to invoke the responsibility of the state at fault.

While article 42 is mainly concerned with invocation of responsibility by an injured state, article 48 regulates invocation of responsibility by a state other than an injured state.[151] It stipulates that besides the injured state, any state is entitled to invoke the responsibility of another state if the breached obligation is owed to a group of states or the international community as a whole.[152] It is stated in the Commentary that article 48 complements article 42 and regulates invocation of responsibility when a state 'is acting not in its individual capacity by reason of having suffered injury, but in its capacity as a member of a group of States to which the obligation is owed, or indeed as a member of the

148 On the history of standing in the general interest, see ibid 48–49.

149 Article 42, ARSIWA.

150 ARSIWA Commentary, p. 117.

151 For a discussion on individual and general legal interests, see Tams, *Enforcing Obligations Erga Omnes in International Law* (n 147) 40–47.

152 Article 48, ARSIWA.

international community as a whole.'[153] As the ARSIWA Commentary points out, international law goes beyond bilateral obligations and also protects interests that states owe to the international community as a whole.[154] After having rejected standing in the general interest in the case of South West Africa,[155] only four years later, the ICJ changed its position and declared in the Barcelona Traction case that:

> an essential distinction should be drawn between the obligations of a State towards the international community as a whole, and those arising vis-à-vis another State in the field of diplomatic protection. By their very nature the former are the concern of all States. In view of the importance of the rights involved, all States can be held to have a legal interest in their protection; they are obligations *erga omnes*.[156]

For the human rights expansionist discourse, the identification of obligations as *erga omnes* was of vital importance. The *erga omnes* character of human rights obligations is very closely related to the non-reciprocal character of human rights treaties. As explained above, human rights treaties do not create contractual obligations, but states undertake to respect fundamental rights for individuals living within their jurisdiction. In that sense, states do not have a direct interest toward one another when they sign human rights treaties. According to this exceptionalist approach, it is the international community as a whole that has an interest in the protection of human rights. This was confirmed by the ICJ in the Barcelona Traction case where the Court cited

153 ARSIWA Commentary, p. 126.

154 ARSIWA Commentary, p. 126–128.

155 In 1966, the Court had refused to recognise standing in the general interest and stated: 'For these reasons the Court, bearing in mind that the rights of the Applicants must be determined by reference to the character of the system said to give rise to them, considers that the "necessity" argument falls to the ground for lack of verisimilitude in the context of the economy and philosophy of that system. Looked at in another way moreover, the argument amounts to a plea that the Court should allow the equivalent of an "actio popularis", or right resident in any member of a community to take legal action in vindication of a public interest. But although a right of this kind may be known to certain municipal systems of law, it is not known to international law as it stands at present: nor is the Court able to regard it as imported by the "general principles of law" referred to in Article 38, paragraph 1 (c), of its Statute.' in ICJ Reports, South West Africa Cases (Ethiopia v. South Africa, Liberia v. South Africa) Second Phase, Judgment, p. 47, para. 88.

156 Barcelona Traction Heat, Light, and Power Co (Belgium v Spain), Second Phase, ICJ Reports 1970, p. 32, para 33.

'principles and rules concerning the basic rights of the human person, including protection from slavery and racial discrimination' as examples of *erga omnes* obligations in international law.[157] Several references in the Commentary of ARSIWA to Barcelona Traction demonstrates that the judgment has formed the pillar for the codification of article 48 and how states can invoke responsibility when they are not the injured state.

In the East Timor case, the Court further added self-determination to the list of rights that create obligations *erga omnes*. The Court stated:

> In the Court's view, Portugal's assertion that the right of peoples to self-determination, as it evolved from the Charter and from United Nations practice, has an *erga omnes* character, is irreproachable. The principle of self-determination of peoples has been recognized by the United Nations Charter and in the jurisprudence of the Court (…); it is one of the essential principles of contemporary international law.[158]

It can be noted that the recognition of human rights as rights creating obligations *erga omnes* stems from the special character of human rights obligations. As indicated by the ICJ in its Genocide Advisory Opinion:

> the contracting States do not have any interests of their own; they merely have, one and all, a common interest, namely the accomplishment of those high purposes which are the *raison d'être* of the convention. Consequently, in a convention of this type, one cannot speak of individual advantages and disadvantages to States, or of the maintenance of a perfect contractual balance between rights and duties.[159]

In this famous passage, the ICJ did not expand on how the non-reciprocal character of human rights obligations affect the standing of states.[160] Nevertheless, it is possible to deduce from the reasoning of the Court that the injury caused

157 Barcelona Traction Heat, Light, and Power Co (Belgium v Spain), Second Phase, ICJ Reports 1970, p. 32, para 34.

158 East Timor (Portugal v. Australia), Judgment, ICJ Reports 1995, p. 90, para. 29. In the same vein, see also Legal Consequences of the Construction of a Wall in the Occupied Palestinian Territory, Advisory Opinion, ICJ Reports 2004, para. 136, Legal Consequences of the Separation of the Chagos Archipelago from Mauritius in 1965, Advisory Opinion, ICJ Reports 2019, para. 180.

159 Genocide Advisory Opinion, 23.

160 Tams, *Enforcing Obligations Erga Omnes in International Law* (n 147) 50.

by a human rights violation goes beyond a bilateral understanding and that in this specific field, we cannot content with the concept of individual injury. When a state violates its human rights obligations, the primary party to make an allegation is an individual victim rather than a state since other signatories to the treaty do not have a direct injury.[161] Conversely, it can also be argued that each and every state has an interest in the protection of fundamental rights. In that sense, while the direct victim of a human rights violation is an individual, states can still be said to have standing against the state at fault. This stems from the *erga omnes* character of human rights obligations which serve to establish a set of values, rather than individual interests. In that sense, *erga omnes* obligations, such as human rights obligations, help to constitutionalise international law by providing a common set of values.[162]

As the UN Special Rapporteur, James Crawford argued in his Third Report that it is necessary to differentiate between how states can respond to individual human rights violations and gross or systematic human rights violations. He stated that '[i]t may be that third States are considered as having more extensive rights to intervene or to respond to systematic breaches of human rights than they might have in cases of individual breach'.[163] He advocated that since human rights obligations do not create reciprocal obligations among signatory states, when there is a violation each state should not be in a position to make a claim 'in the first instance'.[164] While all states have a legitimate concern for the fulfilment of human rights obligations, Crawford was of the opinion that this does not place states which are not specially affected by the violation at the same position with an individual who is the direct victim. This view, however, is not reflected in the last draft of ARSIWA or discussed in its Commentary. In that sense, there is no peculiar difference regarding standing between an individual or other signatory states when it comes to violations of human rights treaties.

161 Brilmayer, 'From 'Contract' to 'Pledge': The Structure of International Human Rights Agreements', (n 14) 177. It should be noted that states can protect their nationals from violations of human rights law through diplomatic protection, see Annemarieke Vermeer-Künzli, 'Diplomatic Protection as a Source of Human Rights Law' in Shelton (ed.), *The Oxford Handbook of International Human Rights Law* (Oxford University Press 2013).

162 Jost Delbrück, 'A Fresh Look at Humanitarian Intervention under the Authority of the United Nations', (1992) 67 Indiana Law Journal 35. On the dangers of a right to *actio popularis* regarding human rights and how this can turn into an apology for imperialism, see Koskenniemi, 'The Pull of the Mainstream', (n 63) 1960.

163 Third Report, James Crawford p. 30, para. 87.

164 Third Report, James Crawford p. 30, para. 88.

It is only in 2012 that the ICJ applied the concept of *erga omnes* in relation to a human rights obligation in a dispute. In the case of Obligation to Prosecute or Extradite, the Court ruled that all state parties to the Convention against Torture had a legal interest in the fulfilment of the obligations created by the Convention. While the Court underlined that the Convention created obligations *erga omnes partes*, meaning that it is only parties to the Convention who had an interest in the protection of the Convention obligations, it accepted that a state does not have to demonstrate a direct injury to prove its standing before the Court. It stated:

> As stated in its Preamble, the object and purpose of the Convention is "to make more effective the struggle against torture ... throughout the world". The States parties to the Convention have a common interest to ensure, in view of their shared values, that acts of torture are prevented and that, if they occur, their authors do not enjoy impunity ... All the other States parties have a common interest in compliance with these obligations by the State in whose territory the alleged offender is present. That common interest implies that the obligations in question are owed by any State party to all the other States parties to the Convention. All the States parties "have a legal interest" in the protection of the rights involved ... These obligations may be defined as "obligations *erga omnes partes*" in the sense that each State party has an interest in compliance with them in any given case.
>
> The common interest in compliance with the relevant obligations under the Convention against Torture implies the entitlement of each State party to the Convention to make a claim concerning the cessation of an alleged breach by another State party. If a special interest were required for that purpose, in many cases no State would be in the position to make such a claim. It follows that any State party to the Convention may invoke the responsibility of another State party with a view to ascertaining the alleged failure to comply with its obligations *erga omnes partes*.[165]

In general international law, it is only signatory states to a treaty that would have a right to compel the other party to respect its obligations. Furthermore, it is beyond international law's purview to monitor through bodies composed of state representatives or independent experts whether states do

165 Obligation to Prosecute or Extradite (Belgium v Senegal), Judgment, ICJ Reports 2012, pp. 449–450, para. 68–69.

comply with their treaty obligations. As regards human rights law, the *erga omnes* character of human rights obligations is also reflected in the protection mechanisms established at the global and regional level. The UN has set up various monitoring mechanisms to supervise the human rights situation in states. For instance, the Human Rights Council conducts universal periodic review to evaluate the human rights situation in UN member states. Each state is under a duty to report to the Council about the steps it took to improve its human rights record. In addition, several UN human rights treaties have their own monitoring mechanisms which require states to report to the respective Committee about the implementation of the treaty. Human rights monitoring mechanisms established at the universal level work in parallel with regional mechanisms set up by the Organization of American States, African Union and the Council of Europe. These various monitoring mechanisms showcase how each and every state has an interest in the genuine implementation of human rights even if they did not suffer a direct injury.

3.2.4 The Constitutional Nature

In international law, constitutional law analogies are abundant.[166] It is commonplace for the international legal discourse to draw on the long-established pedigree of domestic law concepts to elaborate on the international legal system. It has been discussed at length whether the UN Charter constitutes a constitution for international law,[167] whether the WTO constitutes a

166 See generally, Laurence R Helfer, 'Constitutional Analogies in the International Legal System', (2003) 37 Loyola of Los Angeles Law Review 193, Erika De Wet, 'The International Constitutional Order', (2006) 55 International & Comparative Law Quarterly 51–76, Jan Klabbers, Anne Peters, and Geir Ulfstein, *The Constitutionalization of International Law* (Oxford University Press 2009), Christine E.J. Schwöbel, *Global Constitutionalism in International Legal Perspective* (Brill 2011), Christian Walter, 'Constitutionalizing (Inter)National Governance-Possibilities for and Limits to the Development of an International Constitutional Law', (2001) 44 German Yearbook of International Law 170, Joseph Weiler, 'The Geology of International Law: Governance, Democracy and Legitimacy', (2004) 46 ZAÖRV 547–62.

167 See Bardo Fassbender, 'The United Nations Charter as Constitution of the International Community', (1998) 36 Columbia Journal of Transnational Law 529, Pierre-Marie Dupuy, 'The Constitutional Dimension of the Charter of the United Nations Revisited', *Max Planck Yearbook of United Nations Law Online*, 1/1 (1997).

constitutional order,[168] or whether international law needs constitutionalisation.[169] Constitutional approaches to international law have provided ample discursive tools to diversify the theoretical landscape of the field and in equal measure faced severe criticisms.[170] The comparison between domestic constitutional law concepts and human rights has also been generously used to create new discursive moves for the latter.[171] International human rights law pursues an expansionist discursivity by oscillating between an attachment to general international law and a move away from it. In its exceptionalist approach, it borrows from domestic law concepts that help to differentiate human rights obligations from general international law obligations. The constitutional nature of human rights law has been another favourable argument to justify the creation of new discursive moves for this expansionist discourse.

International human rights and constitutional rights differ considerably when it comes to their source of authority, legitimacy, normative foundation and institutional supervision.[172] It is, however, possible to draw on an anal-

168 Ernst-Ulrich Petersmann, 'The WTO Constitution and Human Rights', (2000) 3 Journal of International Economic Law 19–25, Jeffrey L Dunoff, 'Constitutional Conceits: The WTO's 'Constitution' and the Discipline of International Law', (2006) 17 European Journal of International Law 647–75, Deborah Z Cass, *The Constitutionalization of the World Trade Organization: Legitimacy, Democracy, and Community in the International Trading System* (Oxford University Press 2005).

169 Jeffrey L Dunoff and Joel P Trachtman (eds.), *Ruling the World?: Constitutionalism, International Law, and Global Governance* (Cambridge University Press 2009), Klabbers, Peters, and Ulfstein, *The Constitutionalization of International Law* (n 166).

170 Nico Krisch, *Beyond Constitutionalism: The Pluralist Structure of Postnational Law* (Oxford University Press 2010), Alec Stone Sweet, 'Constitutionalism, Legal Pluralism, and International Regimes', (2009) 16 Indiana Journal of Global Legal Studies 621–45, Alexander Somek, 'The Concept of 'Law' in Global Administrative Law: A Reply to Benedict Kingsbury', (2009) 20 European Journal of International Law 985–95. Alexander Somek, 'Kelsen Lives', (2007) 18 European Journal of International Law 409–51, Jean d'Aspremont, 'The Foundations of the International Legal Order', (2007) 18 Finnish Yearbook of International Law 219–255, Wouter Werner, 'The Never-Ending Closure: Constitutionalism and International Law' in Nicholas Tsagourias (ed.), *Transnational Constitutionalism: International and European Perspectives* (Cambridge University Press 2007) 329–367, Martti Koskenniemi, 'Constitutionalism as Mindset: Reflections on Kantian Themes About International Law and Globalization', (2006) 8 Theoretical Inquiries in Law 9–36, Koskenniemi, 'The Fate of Public International Law: Between Technique and Politics', (n 90), Jan Klabbers, 'Constitutionalism Lite', (2004) 1 International Organizations Law Review 31–58, David Kennedy, 'The International Style in Postwar Law and Policy', (1994) Utah Law Review 7–103.

171 For a comparison between American constitutional rights and human rights, see Louis Henkin, 'Constitutional Rights and Human Rights', (1978) 13 *Harvard Civil Rights-Civil Liberties Law Review*, 633.

172 Neuman, 'Human Rights and Constitutional Rights: Harmony and Dissonance', (n 56) 1876–7.

ogy between the two sets of rights if one desires to expand the human rights law. The constitutional nature of human rights law is used for two discursive patterns. First, based on an analogy with the function and substance of constitutional law, claims are often made that human rights obligations have a constitutional nature and differ from obligations of a general international law nature. This analogy primarily relies on the function performed by human rights and constitutional rights. They both aim to limit the power of the state and dictate minimal standards that should guide all other legal regulations. Another important similarity between human rights and constitutional rights has to do with their substance.[173] When the content of a general human rights treaty such as the ICCPR or ECHR is compared with any constitution containing fundamental rights, it can be observed that they contain similar provisions. While the range and scope of rights might differ, several constitutions will protect the most basic civil rights such as the right to life, the prohibition of torture and slavery, the freedom of expression, assembly and association and to some extent economic and social rights, including the right to health, education and work. In that sense, underlining the similarity of human rights and constitutional rights by drawing on their function and substance becomes an effective tool to pull the former away from the realm of general international law.

It is also argued that regional human rights treaties such as the European Convention on Human Rights, the American Convention on Human Rights or the African Charter on Human and Peoples' Rights represent more than a collection of fundamental rights for their respective jurisdictions. They rather constitute a public order in their region and determine the minimal standards that states should abide by. The European Court of Human Rights has affirmed in several judgments that the European Convention on Human Rights has a constitutional character for the European public order.[174] In the case of Loizidou v. Turkey, the Court evaluated the permissibility of reservations entered by the respondent government. It affirmed that permitting the territorial reservation of states would create 'separate regimes of enforcement of Convention obligations' and that this would 'diminish the effectiveness of the Convention as a constitutional instrument of European public order.'[175]

173 Gardbaum, 'Human Rights as International Constitutional Rights', (n 58) 751.

174 In the same vein, see also Klabbers, Peters, and Ulfstein, *The Constitutionalization of International Law* (n 166) 218.

175 Loizidou v Turkey (Preliminary Objections) (1995) 20 EHRR 99, para. 75. The constitutional character of the ECHR for a European public order goes hand in hand with the subsidiarity of the Convention system, see Alastair Mowbray, 'Subsidiarity and the European Convention on Human Rights', (2015) 15 Human Rights Law Review 313–41, Robert Spano,

When evaluating the contribution made by the European and American regional human rights regimes, Judge Cançado Trindade stated that '[t]he work of the Inter-American and European Courts of Human Rights has indeed contributed to the creation of an international *ordre public* based upon the respect for human rights in all circumstances'.[176] At a universal level, it is common to refer to the collection of the Universal Declaration of Human Rights (UDHR), the International Covenant on Civil and Political Rights (ICCPR) and the International Covenant on Economic, Social and Political Rights as the Bill of Rights.[177] The analogy with constitutional law is often made to claim that human rights are not merely a set of treaty obligations agreed by states, but rather they constitute a general legal framework that constitutes the basis upon which all other rights and obligations should be built.

The European Court of Human Rights created the doctrine of margin of appreciation to balance out the constitutional character of the European Convention. International human rights provide certain minimal standards that should be respected by states. The way these standards will be implemented depend considerably on the historical, cultural and legal characteristics of each state. The ECtHR relies on the margin of appreciation when it is confronted with a controversial case where there is no European consensus on how the Convention should be interpreted and applied. In particular, when the case involves an issue that relates to national security, balancing of different rights, protection of public morals, implementation of social and economic policies, the Court defers to the national judge who is better suited to rule on these sensitive questions.[178] This allows a certain discretion to the national

---

'The Future of the European Court of Human Rights – Subsidiarity, Process-Based Review and the Rule of Law', (2015) 15 Human Rights Law Review 473–94, Thomas Kleinlein, 'The Procedural Approach of the European Court of Human Rights: Between Subsidiarity and Dynamic Evolution', (2019) 68 International & Comparative Law Quarterly, 91–110, Dean Spielmann, 'Allowing the Right Margin: The European Court of Human Rights and the National Margin of Appreciation Doctrine: Waiver or Subsidiarity of European Review?', (2012) 14 Cambridge Yearbook of European Legal Studies, 381–418, De Souza Rbeiro v France, ECHR, 22689/07, 13 December 2012.

176 IACtHR, Caesar Case, Series C, No. 123 (2005) (separate opinion of Judge Cançado Trindade), para. 7.

177 See Human Rights Committee, General Comment 26, UN Doc CCPR/C/21/Rev.1/Add.8/Rev.1 (8 December 1997), para. 3.

178 For a critic of the margin of appreciation, see Jan Kratochvíl, 'The Inflation of the Margin of Appreciation by the European Court of Human Rights', (2011) 29 Netherlands Quarterly of Human Rights 324–57. See also the dissenting opinion of Judge De Meyer in Z v. Finland (1997) 25 EHRR, 371/2 (1997).

authority in the implementation of the Convention which goes hand in hand with the Court's supervision.

The IACtHR and the ECtHR have closely followed each other's jurisprudence and borrowed several tools of interpretation from each other. Yet, this was not the case for the much acclaimed doctrine of the margin of appreciation that was developed by the latter. While the European Court prefers to rely on the margin of appreciation doctrine regarding cases where there is no European consensus, the American Court adopted a more autonomous approach in the interpretation of its human rights convention. In comparison to its European counterpart, the IACtHR acts more like a constitutional court which has the final say in the interpretation of the American Convention.[179] The American Court has so far not applied the margin of appreciation doctrine and has delivered some judgments that have been qualified as too progressive by states.[180] In addition to denying the discretionary power of states in the implementation of certain provisions of the Convention, the Court has been more generous than any other regional human rights court to declare that some provisions of the Convention are *jus cogens* norms.[181] Neuman argued that this progressive approach of the Court that identifies *jus cogens* norms that are universally applicable is against the principle of state voluntarism.[182] In that sense, the American Court has not been shy to act like a constitutional court to have the final say in the interpretation of the Convention rights.

The approach of the Human Rights Committee has been more in line with the approach of the American Court rather than its European counterpart. In its General Comment 34, the Committee stated that it 'reserves to itself an assessment of whether, in a given situation, there may have been circumstances which made a restriction of freedom of expression necessary. In this regard, the Committee recalled that the scope of this freedom is not to

179 For instance, this is how the IACtHR decided in its Advisory Opinion OC-24/17 (2017) that prohibition of same-sex marriage is against the prohibition of discrimination. When the ECtHR was confronted with the same question in the case of Chapin and Charpentier v. France (2016), it ruled that national states should enjoy a margin of appreciation and did not find a violation of the European Convention. See Nicolás Carrillo-Santarelli, 'Gender Identity, and Equality and Non-Discrimination of Same Sex Couples' (2018) 112 American Journal of International Law 479.

180 Andreas Follesdal, 'Exporting the Margin of Appreciation: Lessons for the Inter-American Court of Human Rights', (2017) 15 International Journal of Constitutional Law 359–71, 361–62.

181 On forced disappearance, see Goiburú Case, Inter-American Court of Human Rights, Series C, No. 153 (2006), para 93, extrajudicial execution, see Gómez Paquiyauri Brothers Case, Inter-American Court of Human Rights, Series C, No. 110 (2004), para. 76.

182 Gerald L Neuman, 'Import, Export, and Regional Consent in the Inter-American Court of Human Rights', (2008) 19 European Journal of International Law 101–23, 117.

be assessed by reference to a 'margin of appreciation'.[183] In other words, the Human Rights Committee sees itself as the final organ to decide on the compliance of measures adopted by states, rather than adopting a more relativist approach in the implementation of the Covenant.

3.2.5 Withdrawal

While some human rights treaties expressly determine under which conditions states can withdraw from the treaty, others are silent on the matter. It is controversial whether states can withdraw from a human rights treaty when there is no provision on withdrawal. In general international law, states are allowed to withdraw from a treaty under certain conditions.[184] This is regulated in articles 54–56 of the VCLT. According to article 54 of the VCLT, parties to an international law treaty can terminate or withdraw from the treaty either in accordance with the provisions of the treaty or by the consent of all the parties. This is the case for example with regard to the European Convention on Human Rights which regulates in article 58 how states can denounce the treaty. Greece, for instance, denounced the application of the ECHR between 1969 and 1974 following the military coup of 1967.[185] In the same line, article 78 of the American Convention on Human Rights determine the modalities for denunciation.[186] This article has already been put in practice when Trinidad and Tobago[187] in 1998 and Venezuela[188] in 2012 withdrew from the Convention.

---

183 Human Rights Committee, General Comment 34, CCPR/C/GC/34, 12 September 2011, para. 36.

184 See generally, Laurence Helfer, 'Exiting Treaties', (2005) 91 Virginia Law Review 1579, Yogesh Tyagi, 'The Denunciation of Human Rights Treaties', (2009) 79 The British Yearbook of International Law 86, Linos-Alexander Sicilianos, 'The Relationship between Reprisals and Denunciation or Suspension of a Treaty', (1993) 4 European Journal of International Law 341.

185 Council of Europe (Committee of Ministers) (12 December 1969) CM (69) PV 4, 20.

186 For an advisory opinion of the Inter-American Court of Human Rights on withdrawal from the Convention, see Advisory Opinion OC-26/20, available at: www.corteidh.or.cr/docs/opiniones/seriea_26_esp.pdf. See also Sylvia Steininger, 'Don't Leave Me This Way: Regulating Treaty Withdrawal in the Inter-American Human Rights System' EJIL: Talk! (5 March 2021), available at: www.ejiltalk.org/dont-leave-me-this-way-regulating-treaty-withdrawal-in-the-inter-american-human-rights-system/.

187 Trinidad and Tobago: Notice to Denounce the American Convention on Human Rights (26 May 1998), available at: www.oas.org/dil/treaties_b-32_american_convention_on_human_rights_sign.htm#Trinidad%20and%20Tobago. See also Christina Cerna, 'Denunciation of the American Convention on Human Rights: The Trinidad & Tobago Death Penalty cases' available at: www.corteidh.or.cr/tablas/r31601.pdf.

188 Venezuela: Notice to Denounce the American Convention on Human Rights (6 September 2012), available at: www.oas.org/dil/esp/Nota_Republica_Bolivariana_de_Venezuela_al_SG_OEA.PDF. See also Diego German Mejia-Lemos, 'Venezuela's Denunciation of the American Convention on Human Rights' 17 (1) AJIL Insights

Several UN human rights treaties, including the Convention against Torture, the Convention on the Rights of the Child, and the Convention on the Elimination of Racial Discrimination, regulate how states can denounce the treaty.

Withdrawal from human rights treaties is perceived, however, as a sensitive matter since it can leave individuals without the protection of fundamental rights. While some human rights treaties allow denunciation, others adopt a more restrictive approach. The African Charter on Human and Peoples' Rights does not recognise the possibility to denounce the treaty. There has been a controversy as to whether states can withdraw their consent recognising the competence of the African Court on Human and Peoples' Rights to receive applications from individuals and NGO's. Article 34 of the Protocol to the African Court on Human and Peoples' Rights prescribes that states have to make a declaration recognising the Court's competence to receive applications from individuals and NGO's. The article does not indicate whether states can withdraw their declaration. Rwanda was the first state in 2016 to declare its withdrawal of the declaration recognising the Court's competence.[189] Rwanda argued that its declaration was effective immediately and that the Court did not have jurisdiction to give a decision on pending cases. This claim was rejected by the Court in its Ingabire Victoire Umuhoza v. the Republic of Rwanda judgment where the Court declared that the declaration of withdrawal was effective only a year after its submission and that it would have no legal effect on ongoing cases.[190] The Court recognised the ability of states to withdraw their consent even if the Protocol was silent about the matter. Nevertheless, it is noteworthy that the Court interpreted article 34 in favour of a considerable delay for the declaration of withdrawal to be effective which is in line with article 56(2) of the VCLT.

The Human Rights Committee had to take a position regarding the ICCPR when North Korea, the first state to make such a request, expressed its desire to withdraw from the treaty. In 1998, North Korea wanted to withdraw from the ICCPR due to the Human Rights Committee's harsh criticism about its

(9 January 2013), Julian Ku, 'Venezuela Formally Withdraws from American Convention on Human Rights, Blames the U.S.' Opinio Juris (11 September 2013), available at: http://opiniojuris.org/2013/09/11/venezuela-formally-withdraws-american-convention-human-rights-blames-u-s/.

189 Rwanda's withdrawal was followed by Tanzania in 2019, and by the Republic of Benin and Côte d'Ivoire in 2020.

190 African Court on Human and Peoples' Rights, Ingabire Victoire Umuhoza v. the Republic of Rwanda, App. No. 003/2014 (24 November 2017). See also Harrison Mbori, 'Ingabire Victoire Umuhoza v. The Republic of Rwanda' (2018) 112 American Journal of International Law 713.

human rights record.[191] The Sub-Commission on Prevention of Discrimination and Protection of Minorities wanted to adopt a resolution criticising the non-fulfilment of the ICCPR obligations by North Korea. To prevent the adoption of this Resolution, North Korea replied by a letter indicating that the resolution was politically motivated and that they would withdraw from the ICCPR if it was adopted.[192] The ICCPR does not include an article on denunciation. In case the treaty is silent about termination, denunciation or withdrawal, the VCLT provides in article 56 that states can only denounce the treaty if this can be inferred from the intention of the parties or if this is implied by the nature of the treaty. The first reaction regarding North Korea's request came from the UN Secretary-General. Since the Covenant was silent on denunciation, the issue was transferred to the Secretary-General as the depository of the Covenant. The opinion of the Secretary-General was in the negative and it was affirmed that the withdrawal of a party would be possible only if all parties to the treaty agreed to it.[193] Due to the uncertainty on the possibility of denunciation of the ICCPR, the Human Rights Committee decided to draft a General Comment.[194] Only a year after the request made by North Korea, the Human Rights Committee published General Comment 26 and took a much firmer position than the one adopted by the Secretary-General. In its General Comment 26, the Human Rights Committee expressly stated the silence of the ICCPR was intentional and that the exceptions provided in article 56 of the VCLT would not be applicable.[195] The Committee claimed that the silence of the treaty could not be seen as a 'mere oversight'. In order to justify its interpretation, it presented several reasons. First, while article 41(2) of the Covenant allowed states to withdraw their consent regarding the Committee's competence to receive inter-state applications, withdrawal from the treaty was not expressly regulated. Second, the drafters also allowed states to withdraw from the Optional Protocol which was adopted at the same period as the ICCPR.

191 Elizabeth Evatt, 'Democratic People's Republic of Korea and the ICCPR: Denunciation as an Exercise of the Right of Self-Defence?', (1999) 5 Australian Journal of Human Rights 215–24.

192 Letter dated 18 August 1997 from the Chargé d'affaires a.i. of the Permanent Mission of the Democratic People's Republic of Korea to the United Nations Office in Geneva addressed to the Chairman of the forty-ninth session of the Sub-Commission on Prevention of Discrimination and Protection of Minorities, UN Doc E/CN.4/Sub.2/1997/43.

193 Ed Bates, 'Avoiding Legal Obligations', (2008) 57 The International and Comparative Law Quarterly 755, Laurence Helfer, 'Terminating Treaties' in *The Oxford Guide to Treaties* Duncan Hollies ed (Oxford University Press 2012) 639–40.

194 Evatt, 'Democratic People's Republic of Korea and the ICCPR: Denunciation as an Exercise of the Right of Self-Defence?', (n 191) 217.

195 Human Rights Committee, General Comment 26, UN Doc CCPR/C/21/Rev.1/Add.8/Rev.1 (8 December 1997).

Third, the International Convention on the Elimination of All Forms of Racial Discrimination, which was adopted only a year before the ICCPR, did recognise denunciation. These comparisons led the Committee to conclude that it was a deliberate choice of the drafters not to allow states to withdraw from the ICCPR. In addition to these comparisons, the Committee also touched on the constitutional character of the ICCPR to justify why states cannot denounce it. It stated that the UDHR, ICCPR and ICESCR are often referred to as the International Bill of Human Rights and therefore 'the Covenant does not have a temporary character typical of treaties where a right of denunciation is deemed to be admitted, notwithstanding the absence of a specific provision to that effect.'[196]

3.2.6 Succession

Emergence and disappearance of new entities bring about important changes that have the potential to disrupt the stability of international affairs. Succession rules aim to provide a legal framework to regulate the fate of predecessor and successor states in relation to their treaties, debts, archives, public property etc. In particular, succession to international treaties is a complicated matter that depends on several variables. Regulation of treaty relations following succession will depend on a number of factors, including the existence of a devolution agreement, unilateral statements made by predecessor or successor states, the nature of treaties, the nature of succession whether it is absorption, merger, dissolution, newly independent state or separation from another state. In general international law, state succession and its effects on treaties are regulated mainly by customary rules and the 1978 Vienna Convention on Succession of States in Respect of Treaties. During the preparation of the 1978 Vienna Convention, the ILC discussed whether a newly independent state should be bound by multilateral treaties of a law-making character.[197] It was decided that there was no unequivocal and consistent state practice in that regard and therefore, no special rule was prescribed for treaties of a law-making character.[198]

Succession to treaties has been another site for the successful invocation of the special nature of human rights obligations. Once again, the HRC challenged the ILC regarding the way in which succession to treaties was regulated

196 Human Rights Committee, General Comment 26, UN Doc CCPR/C/21/Rev.1/Add.8/Rev.1 (8 December 1997), para 3.

197 ILC, Yearbook of the International Law Commission (1974), Volume II, Part I, UN Doc. A/CN.4/SER.A/1974/Add.1, p. 43.

198 Ibid.

in general international law. The lack of a special status for human rights treaties in the Vienna Convention on Succession of States in Respect of Treaties was addressed and, in a sense, filled by the HRC with a progressive interpretation of human rights obligations. During the dissolution of Yugoslavia, the HRC played an essential role in bestowing human rights treaties a separate position that required distinct rules from general international law treaties. In 1992, by taking a proactive step, the HRC requested that Bosnia and Herzegovina, Croatia and the Federal Republic of Yugoslavia (Serbia and Montenegro) submit a report to the Committee in order to explain how rights enshrined in the ICCPR were protected during the conflicts.[199] The Chairman of the HRC indicated that 'the Committee was authorized to request reports on the basis of its previously held position that, despite the legal problems involved in the succession of States, there was no reason to presume that successor states would not continue to apply human rights treaties'.[200] At the time when the HRC took this decision, these three states had not yet made any statements about whether they would continue to be a party to the ICCPR. Nonetheless, the HRC deemed itself competent to make such a request and indicated that people who enjoyed the guarantees provided by the ICCPR under former Yugoslavia, still were entitled to the same protection. After the reports were submitted by the three states, in its comments adopted after its consideration of the reports, the HRC noted that by submitting the reports and sending a delegation before it, states confirmed their succession to the ICCPR.[201] In 1997, the HRC adopted General Comment 26 on the continuity of obligations to the ICCPR and reiterated the same approach.[202] The General Comment indicated that human rights belong to the people of the state party and that once these rights were recognised by states to the people, they devolved with the territory regardless of any governmental change or state succession.[203]

In the same line with the HRC, the Commission on Human Rights adopted a resolution in 1993 to urge successor states to accept that they will continue to be bound by the human rights treaties that applied to their territory before

199 Human Rights Committee, 46th Session, 5 November 1992, UN Doc CCPR/C/SR.1178/Add.1.

200 Ibid.

201 Human Rights Committee, Comments on the Republic of Bosnia-Herzegovina UN Doc CCPR/C/79/Add.14, Comments of the HRC on Croatia UN Doc CCPR/C/79/Add.15, Comments of the HRC on the Federal Republic of Yugoslavia (Serbia and Montenegro) UN Doc CCPR/C/79/Add.16.

202 Human Rights Committee, General Comment 26, 8 December 1997, UN Doc CCPR/C/21/Rev.1/Add.8/Rev.1.

203 Ibid para. 4.

succession.[204] It is noteworthy that it was not only the independent experts of the HRC who were adamant in providing a long-lasting life to human rights treaties, but the state representatives of the Commission defended that once fundamental rights embodied in a treaty have been recognised to people living in a certain territory, they should continue to enjoy the same level of protection. In 1994, the chairpersons of treaty bodies also affirmed that successor states were automatically bound by human rights treaties that were applicable in their territory since the day of independence without any necessity to make a declaration to that end.[205]

The dissolution of Yugoslavia and its impact on succession to international human rights treaties was discussed at the ICJ in the Genocide Convention case. In his separate opinion for the preliminary objections, Judge Shahabuddeen declared that

> the object and purpose of the Genocide Convention required parties to observe it in such a way as to avoid the creation of such a break in the protection which it afforded. The Convention could not be read as meaning that a Party, which was bound under the Convention to apply its jurisdictional provisions for the protection of the "human groups" inhabiting a given area, was allowed to regard itself as liberated from those provisions in relation to a successor State by reason of the fact that that particular area was now comprised within the territory of the successor State; such a party would continue to be bound by those provisions in relation to other parties in respect of the same "human groups" while being inconsistently free in relation to the successor State within whose territory breaches of the Convention are allegedly being perpetrated by it.
>
> To effectuate its object and purpose, the Convention would fall to be construed as implying the expression of a unilateral undertaking by each party to the Convention to treat successor States as continuing as from independence any status which the predecessor State had as a party to the Convention.[206]

204 The UN Commission on Human Rights, Resolution 1993/23, 5 March 1993. In the same line, see also the UN Commission on Human Rights, Resolution 1994/16, 25 February 1994.

205 The UN Commission on Human Rights, 51st session, 28 November 1994, UN Doc. E/CN.4/1995/80, p. 4.

206 Application of the Convention on the Prevention and Punishment of the Crime of Genocide (Bosnia and Herzegovina v Federal Republic of Yugoslavia), Preliminary Objections, ICJ Reports 1996, 635–6.

In his separate opinion, Judge Weeramantry presented strong arguments in lengthy detail in favour of automatic succession to the Genocide Convention. He examined several arguments that can be put forward in order to put aside the clean slate doctrine regarding human rights and humanitarian law treaties. He reiterated that human rights treaties do not protect states' contractual interests toward one another and that obligations arising from human rights treaties protect interests of the international community.[207] He further stated that rather than considering obligations of human rights treaties as a burden on the state, it should be accepted that they bring advantages to the state by allowing it to become part of that treaty system.[208] Another important argument presented by Judge Weeramantry in favour of automatic succession to human rights treaties relies on the importance of global stability: 'A State's guarantees of human rights to its subjects in terms of even such a Covenant as the International Covenant on Civil and Political Rights are thus a matter which does not concern that State alone, but represent a contribution to human dignity and global stability – as distinguished, for example, from a commercial or trading treaty'.[209] He further claimed that it would be 'strange' if people who benefited from the protection of a human rights treaty was left without this protection following a state succession.[210] He therefore argued that it would not be acceptable not to allow automatic succession to international human rights treaties following state succession.

The primary driving force for those who want human rights treaties to devolve with the territory after state succession is the fear that individuals might be left without any human rights protection until the new state accedes to these treaties. This is an issue that can be overcome by the protection provided by fundamental rights that have already become part of customary international law. This, however, does not seem to be an adequate response considering the innovative constructions witnessed in the legal discourse when it comes to succession to human rights treaties. To that end, scholars have long searched for ways to prove that automatic succession to human rights treaties is indeed justified by existing international law rules as well. Kamminga, for instance, is of the view that the reason why human rights treaties continue to apply to successor states stems from the lack of termination clauses in these treaties.[211] He argued that this view was also supported by article 60/5 of the

207 Ibid 646.

208 Ibid 647.

209 Ibid 649.

210 Ibid 649–50.

211 Menno T Kamminga, 'State Succession in Respect of Human Rights Treaties', (1996) 7 European Journal of International Law 472.

VCLT which did not allow termination or suspension of a treaty protecting the human person in response to its breach.[212]

3.2.7 Reservations

Reservations have been one of the most fertile grounds in international law for the expansionist moves at work in the human rights discourse. Reservations to human rights treaties have been extensively studied.[213] The focus here will only be on the expansionist discursive moves that have been deployed to expand human rights. Through a reliance on the different nature of human rights and international law obligations, the discourse has accommodated creative reasonings justifying why this particular regime requires specific discursive moves. Reservations in general international law serve to modify or exclude the legal effect of a treaty provision by which the state does not want to be bound in its entirety. This facilitates the participation of the state into the treaty even if it does not agree with all the provisions and provides some flexibility in international affairs. It is especially an important mechanism in order to increase the number of signatory states in multilateral treaties. Since it is difficult to draft a document that can satisfy a crowded number of states with various interests,

---

212 Ibid.

213 See generally, Ineta Ziemele (ed.), *Reservations to Human Rights Treaties and the Vienna Convention Regime: Conflict, Harmony or Reconciliation* (Martinus Nijhoff Publishers 2004), J.P. Gardner (ed.), *Human Rights as General Norms and a State's Right to Opt Out: Reservations and Objections to Human Rights Conventions* (British Institute of International and Comparative Law 1997), Yogesh Tyagi, 'The Conflict of Law and Policy on Reservations to Human Rights Treaties', (2001) 71 British Yearbook of International Law 181, Roberto Baratta, 'Should Invalid Reservations to Human Rights Treaties Be Disregarded?', (2000) 11 European Journal of International Law, 413–25, Ineta Ziemele and Lāsma Liede, 'Reservations to Human Rights Treaties: From Draft Guideline 3.1. 12 to Guideline 3.1. 5.6', (2013) 24 European Journal of International Law, 1135–52, Henry J Bourguignon, 'The Belilos Case: New Light on Reservations to Multilateral Treaties', (1988) 29 Vanderbilt Journal of Transnational Law 347, Eric Neumayer, 'Qualified Ratification: Explaining Reservations to International Human Rights Treaties', (2007) 36 The Journal of Legal Studies 397–429, Ryan Goodman, 'Human Rights Treaties, Invalid Reservations, and State Consent' in Michael K Addo (ed.), *International Law of Human Rights* (Routledge 2016), William Schabas, 'Reservations to Human Rights Treaties: Time for Innovation and Reform', (1995) 32 Canadian Yearbook of International Law 39, Ed Bates, 'Avoiding Legal Obligations Created by Human Rights Treaties', (2008) 57 International & Comparative Law Quarterly 751–88, Alain Pellet, 'Reservations to Treaties and the Integrity of Human Rights' in Sheeran and Rodley (eds.), *Routledge Handbook of International Human Rights Law* (Routledge 2016), Kasey L Mccall-Smith, 'Severing Reservations', (2014) 63 International & Comparative Law Quarterly 599–634, Alain Pellet and Daniel Müller, 'Reservations to Human Rights Treaties: Not an Absolute Evil', in Ulrich Fastenrath et al. (eds.), *From Bilateralism to Community Interest: Essays in Honour of Bruno Simma* (Oxford University Press 2011).

states are given the opportunity to amend the legal effect of some provisions of a treaty by making a unilateral statement. They can be perceived, however, as a threat to the effective implementation of human rights.[214] It is to prevent the debilitating effect that reservations can have on the integrity of treaties that various ways to create innovative discursive constructions regarding reservations have been attempted and tried out.

According to article 19 of the VCLT, reservations are permissible unless they are prohibited by the treaty or against the object and purpose of the treaty. The former criterion is easily identifiable. It is usually expressly stated in the treaty whether entering reservations or a specified reservation is prohibited. The latter, however, is not a straightforward exercise. Establishing the object and purpose of the treaty and evaluating whether a reservation is compatible with them have obviously been the object of a lot of attention.[215] The intricate practice of determining the object and purpose of the treaty has provided a very convenient discursive justification to expand human rights. In the Advisory Opinion on the Genocide Convention, the ICJ stated that the Convention did not protect individual or reciprocal interests of states but rather a common interest which corresponded to 'high purposes' that constituted the *raison d'être* of the treaty.[216] Regarding the validity of reservations, it further stated that reservations should be compatible with the object and purpose of the treaty.[217] However, it did not explain how the object and purpose of a treaty can be ascertained and who has the authority to determine whether the reservation is compatible with the object and purpose of the treaty.

Human rights monitoring mechanisms have relied on these gaps left by the ICJ and deployed an expansionist reasoning in the interpretation of reservations entered into human rights treaties. In 1994, the Human Rights Committee published General Comment 24 which addressed reservations entered into the ICCPR. In order to fill the gaps and uncertainties surrounding the issue of invalidity of reservations, the Human Rights Committee made some important interpretations that expanded the application of the Covenant on several grounds. It is clear right from the first paragraph of the General Comment that the Committee was concerned about the high

214 Rosalyn Higgins, 'Human Rights: Some Questions of Integrity', (1989) 15 Commonwealth Law Bulletin 598–614. Elizabeth Lijnzaad, *Reservations to Un-Human Rights Treaties: Ratify and Ruin?* (Martinus Nijhoff Publishers 1995).

215 Catherine Redgwell, 'Universality or Integrity? Some Reflections on Reservations to General Multilateral Treaties', (1993) 64 British Yearbook of International Law 245–82, Jan Klabbers, 'Some Problems Regarding the Object and Purpose of Treaties', (1997) 8 Finnish Yearbook of International Law 138–60.

216 Reservations to the Genocide Convention (Advisory Opinion) [1951] ICJ Rep 15, para. 23.

217 Ibid.

number of reservations that states entered into the ICCPR and that the wide scope of certain reservations carried the risk of damaging the effective implementation of the Covenant.[218] It is not surprising, therefore, that the following paragraphs of the General Comment provide some observations with regard to the evaluation of reservations in human rights law that stretch the limits of rules that apply to reservations in general international law mainly established by the VCLT in articles 19–23. The first expansionist move of the Committee came with its statement that reservations entered into provisions that are also part of customary international law would be invalid.[219] In order to illustrate its interpretation, the Committee noted that provisions protecting freedom from arbitrary arrest and detention, freedom of thought, conscience and religion, presumption of innocence, prohibition of execution of pregnant women or children, dissemination of national, racial or religious hatred, the right to self-determination could not be subject to reservations. This allowed the Committee to broaden the scope of application of the ICCPR for a long list of rights that cannot be limited through reservations.

The second expansionist move of the Committee relates to the inapplicability of the VCLT rules on reservations with regard to human rights treaties.[220] The Committee made a bold statement in its interpretation of the VCLT rules on reservations which created an important break away from general international law. It stated that the rules on reservations as embodied in the VCLT 'are inappropriate to address the problem of reservations to human rights treaties. Such treaties, and the Covenant specifically, are not a web of inter-State exchanges of mutual obligations. They concern the endowment of individuals with rights. The principle of inter-State reciprocity has no place, save perhaps in the limited context of reservations to declarations on the Committee's competence.'[221] The Committee highlighted once again the special character of human rights obligations which are primarily about protecting individuals' interests, rather than bilateral interests of states. The special character of

218 Human Rights Committee, General Comment 24, (11 November 1994), UN Doc CCPR/C/21/Rev.1/Add.6, para 1.

219 Ibid para 8.

220 Martin Scheinin, 'Reservations by States under the International Covenant On Civil and Political Rights and its Optional Protocols, and the Practice of the Human Rights Committee' in Ziemele (ed.), *Reservations to Human Rights Treaties and the Vienna Convention Regime: Conflict, Harmony or Reconciliation* (Martinus Nijhoff Publishers 2004) 47.

221 Human Rights Committee, General Comment 24, (11 November 1994), UN Doc CCPR/C/21/Rev.1/Add.6, para 17. In the same line, see Daniel N Hylton, 'Default Breakdown: The Vienna Convention on the Law of Treaties' Inadequate Framework on Reservations', (1994) 27 Vanderbilt Journal of Transnational Law 419.

human rights obligations allowed the Committee to claim that rules of general international law on reservations do not provide an adequate framework for these treaties. The Committee further emphasised that due to the lack of mutual interests, states usually avoided objecting to other states' reservations. This also seems to be a grave concern for the Committee since it affirmed that the lack of objection for a particular reservation does not mean that the reservation is valid.

The third expansionist move of the Committee pertained to its role in the determination of the validity of reservations. In its Advisory Opinion on the Genocide Convention, the ICJ did not clarify who would have the authority to rule on the validity of a reservation. The framework established by the VCLT puts this power mainly in the hands of states, who in their bilateral relations, can object to a reservation entered by a signatory state. The Committee, however, deviated from this approach and declared that it falls within its competence to decide whether a reservation entered to the ICCPR is valid or not.[222] The Committee underlined that since the ICCPR was a human rights treaty, it would not be appropriate to leave this determination to states. The Committee relied on the special nature of human rights obligations and its role as the guardian of the ICCPR to state that the validity of a reservation in relation to the object and purpose of the treaty should be determined objectively. This was met with criticism by the International Law Commission. The ILC objected to this self-proclaimed role of the Committee about the determination of reservations' validity and it noted that it should be up to states to decide whether they think a reservation is valid or not.[223]

The fourth expansionist move of the Committee was about the severability of reservations. The Committee declared that even if the reservation was found to be invalid, this would be severable and that the state would still continue to be a party to the treaty without the benefit of the reservation.[224] This move of the Committee was inspired by the ECtHR's decision in Belilos v. Switzerland where the Court declared that invalid reservations are severable. Severability

---

222 Human Rights Committee, General Comment 24, (11 November 1994), UN Doc CCPR/C/21/Rev.1/Add.6, para 18.

223 ILC, 'Preliminary Conclusions on Reservations to Normative Multilateral Treaties Including Human Rights Treaties', Yearbook of the International Law Commission (1997), vol II, part two, 57.

224 Human Rights Committee, General Comment 24, (11 November 1994), UN Doc CCPR/C/21/Rev.1/Add.6, para 18. In the same line, see Bruno Simma and Gleider Hernandez, 'Legal Consequences of an Impermissible Reservation to a Human Rights Treaty: Where do we Stand?', in Enzo Cannizzaro (ed.), *The Law of Treaties Beyond the Vienna Convention: Essays in Honour of Giorgio Gaja* (Oxford University Press 2011) 60–85.

of invalid reservations from the consent to be bound depends on the existence of a supervisory body which can make such a determination.[225] The HRC relied on its role as the monitoring body of the ICCPR to assume the role to decide not only on the compatibility of reservations with the object and purpose of the treaty but also on the severability of invalid reservations.

When it was published, the observations of the General Comment 24 on the way human rights treaties should be interpreted and applied received severe reactions. The Human Rights Committee provided some very progressive interpretations which derogated from the general rules as embodied in the VCLT. The first backlash came from states who argued that the General Comment 24 was going beyond the intention of signatory states.[226] In addition, the ILC was not contented with the severe rupture that the Committee created between human rights and general international law. In his second report to the ILC, Special Rapporteur Alain Pellet expressed his concern about this rupture created by the HRC by stating that 'the voice of international law' should be heard.[227] Regarding the exclusion of the ILC from such a crucial debate, he noted that 'it would be unfortunate for it not to take part in a discussion which is of concern to the Commission above all'.[228] His assessment was that the rules set by the VCLT did not create serious impediments for the special character of human rights obligations and was adequate to be applied to these treaties as well.[229] This view was adopted in the Preliminary Conclusions of the ILC on Reservations and it was further stated that it must be states determining the compatibility of reservations with the object and purpose of the treaty.[230] The tension between the two bodies was defused when the ILC, the HRC and other UN treaty bodies met in 2007. In this meeting, the ILC conceded that human rights bodies were competent to evaluate the validity of reservations

225 Catherine Redgwell, 'Reservations to Treaties and Human Rights Committee General Comment No. 24 (52)', (1997) 46 International & Comparative Law Quarterly 390–412, 408–9.

226 For the reactions of US and UK see, Report of the Human Rights Committee, Official Records of the GA, 50th Session, Supplement No. 40, Doc. A/50/40, i, Annex VI. For the reaction of France, see Report of the Human Rights Committee, Official Records of the GA, 51st Session, Supplement No. 40, Doc. A/51/40, i, Annex VI.

227 Second Report on Reservations to Treaties by Mr. Alain Pellet, Special Rapporteur, UN Doc A/CN.4/477 and Add.1 (10 May and 13 June 1996), 1996 Yearbook of the International Law Commission vol II, pt 1, para. 62.

228 Ibid.

229 Ibid para. 163.

230 ILC, Report of the International Law Commission on the Work of its Forty-Ninth Session, 12 May–18 July 1997, Official Records of the General Assembly, Fifty-Second Session, Supplement No. 10, UN Doc A/52/10, p. 57.

entered into their respective human rights treaties.[231] What was left unresolved after the meeting was the issue of severability of reservations. The ILC was not convinced that the invalid reservation could be severed from the expression of consent. In order to overcome this disagreement, the ILC and treaty bodies accepted that there should be a 'reservation dialogue' between the reserving state and the treaty bodies when there is a reservation that is likely to be against the object and purpose of the treaty.[232] The ILC's 2011 Guide to Practice on Reservations to Treaties also encourages 'reservation dialogue' but, unlike the HRC, maintains that the VCLT regime is applicable to all international law treaties including human rights treaties.[233] It should be noted that the Guideline does not mention the issue of severability of invalid reservations but creates a rebuttable presumption about invalid reservations and how they will affect the consent of the state to be bound by the treaty. In Guideline 4.5.3., the ILC stated that "[u]nless the author of the invalid reservation has expressed a contrary intention or such an intention is otherwise established, it is considered a contracting State or a contracting organization without the benefit of the reservation."[234] The same Guideline further explains that in case a state does not want to be bound with the treaty without the benefit of the reservation, it has to express this intention within twelve months from the date at which the treaty monitoring body states that the reservation is invalid. This approach of the ILC can be interpreted as finding a middle ground in the controversy where some argued that a state that entered an invalid reservation to a treaty should be bound by it by severing the invalid reservation, and others who contended that a state that entered an invalid reservation to a treaty should not be bound by the treaty.[235]

The ECtHR assessed the validity of reservations first in the case of Belilos v. Switzerland and then elaborated further on the special character of human rights and its impact on reservations entered into the ECHR in the case of Loizidou v. Turkey. First, in the Belilos case the Court discussed whether an

231 ILC, Meeting with Human Rights Bodies, 15 and 16 May 2007, Report prepared by Mr. Alain Pellet, Special Rapporteur, UN Doc. ILC(LIX)/RT/CRP.1.

232 Ibid para. 35.

233 ILC, Guide to Practice on Reservations to Treaties, Yearbook of the International Law Commission, 2011, vol. II, Part Two, Annex. See also, Michael Wood, 'Institutional Aspects of the Guide to Practice on Reservations', (2013) 24 European Journal of International Law 1099–112.

234 ILC, Guide to Practice on Reservations to Treaties, Yearbook of the International Law Commission, 2011, vol. II, Part Two, Annex.

235 Ineta Ziemele and Lāsma Liede, 'Reservations to Human Rights Treaties: From Draft Guideline 3.1. 12 to Guideline 3.1. 5.6', (2013) 24 European Journal of International Law 1135–52.

interpretative declaration could be considered a reservation. The Court underlined that the naming of the declaration was not relevant and that it would evaluate the intention of those who made the declaration to ascertain whether they intended to make an interpretive declaration or a declaration that aimed to modify the legal effect of the Convention.[236] The Court ruled that the declaration was not valid due to its lack of precision and clarity. The Court concluded with a brief explanation that despite the invalidity of Switzerland's reservation, it still had the competence to decide on the merits of the case.[237] The Court did not only provide a novel approach on the severability of human rights reservations from the declaration to recognise the competence of the Court, but it also by-passed article 20(5) of the VCLT which establishes tacit agreement of reservations by states in case they have not voiced an objection within a twelve month period. The Court deemed itself above such a requirement and did not discuss any limitation as to its power to evaluate the compatibility of reservations deposited in relation to the ECHR.[238]

It is in the case of Loizidou v. Turkey that the Court elaborated in more detail on the severability of invalid reservations made to human rights treaties. In this case, the ECtHR had to evaluate whether the reservation entered by Turkey to the ECHR was compatible with the object and purpose of the treaty. When Turkey recognised the competence of the Court to receive individual applications, it entered a reservation *ratione loci* that rejected the Court's jurisdiction for acts performed outside its national territory. The applicant in the case made allegations about the violation of the Convention in Cyprus and therefore the Court had to evaluate whether it had jurisdiction to rule on the merits. It is significant that the ECtHR took this opportunity to demonstrate how it performs a fundamentally different role than the ICJ. The ECtHR distanced itself from the ICJ by underlining two points. First, it stated that the ICJ is competent to hear any dispute that relates to international law wherever they take place in the globe.[239] Second, the ECtHR indicated that the ICJ does not have the exclusive power to supervise a law-making treaty such as the ECHR.[240] By emphasising these two points, the Court went on to declare that due to their different roles and purposes, it is justifiable that their approach

236 Belilos v. Switzerland (1988) ECHR Ser A No 132, 10 EHRR 418, para. 49.

237 Ibid para 60.

238 Redgwell, 'Reservations to Treaties and Human Rights Committee General Comment No. 24 (52)', (n 225) 399.

239 Loizidou v Turkey (Preliminary Objections) (1995) 20 EHRR 99, para. 84.

240 Ibid para. 84.

to the evaluation of reservations is also different.[241] Finally, the Court ruled that on the basis of the character of the Convention and its object and purpose, the reservation *ratione loci* that was entered with the Turkish declaration recognising the Court's competence to receive individual applications was invalid.[242] In its submission to the Court, Turkey claimed that if the Court were to find the reservation to be invalid, this would mean that the declaration as a whole is null and void and that the Court had no competence to receive individual applications against Turkey. Against this argument, the Court made an interpretation that expanded the Convention's scope of application to a great extent. It ruled that despite the invalidity of the reservation *ratione loci*, Turkey's declaration to recognise the competence of the Court to receive individual applications was still valid. This interpretation relied once again on the special character of the Convention. The Court stated that '[i]n addressing this issue the Court must bear in mind the special character of the Convention as an instrument of European public order (*ordre public*) for the protection of individual human beings.'[243] The Court ruled that the invalid reservation *ratione loci* was separable from the rest of the declaration and that the recognition of the competence of the Court to receive individual applications was still valid.[244]

4 The Wide Range of Expansionist Uses of the Sources of International Human Rights Law

It is submitted in this chapter that, for the sake of the expansion of the scope of international human rights law, the discourse has constantly witnessed the resort to a wide variety of adjustments to the doctrine of the sources of international law, which were originally found too rigid from an expansionist perspective. The emancipation from the rigidity of the sources of international law in international human rights law scholarship and practice does certainly

241 Ibid para. 85.

242 Ibid para. 89.

243 Ibid para. 93.

244 Ibid para. 98. The Inter-American Court has taken a similar position with the ECtHR and ruled on several occasions that invalid reservations are severable. See the Inter-American Court of Human Rights, The Effect of Reservations on the Entry into force of the American Convention (arts. 74 and 75), Advisory Opinion OC-2/82 of 24 September 1982, Series A, No. 2, Restrictions to the Death Penalty (arts. 4(2) and 4(4) American Convention on Human Rights), Advisory Opinion OC-3/83 of 8 September 1983, Series A, No. 3.

not, however, constitute a new phenomenon. Ever since the adoption of formal legal rules on international human rights law and thus since the shift from naturalistic to more positivist discursive moves in terms of international human rights law, practice and scholarship have shown a strong inclination to take some brazen liberty with the doctrine of sources of general international law.[245] This chapter provides a few examples of these emancipatory moves in relation to each of the main sources of international law. It will be shown that, in line with the argument developed in previous chapters, these adjustments to the doctrine of the sources of international law (exceptionalism) are always accompanied by a narrative preserving the membership of international human rights law to general international law (generalism). The expansionist use of custom (4.1.), general principles of law (4.2.), and soft law (4.3.) will be discussed. Other source-based expansionists moves are also mentioned (4.4.).

4.1 *Custom*

In international human rights law scholarship and practice, customary international law has proved the most popular law-ascertainment tool when it comes to stretching the scope of international human rights law and 'discovering' new rules for the protection of individuals. It is as if anything that cannot be supported by treaties and which is deemed desirable can, with a bit of effort and creativity, be found in customary law.[246] The reason for the success of custom is not difficult to fathom. Its greater departure from formal discursive moves[247] provides a less constrained creative space and this is why it has been deemed 'irresistible'.[248] Yet, while custom naturally proves an attractive tool for the expansion of international human rights law, the dominant and traditional understanding of custom may not always be fitted for such an expansionist use of this specific source of international law.[249] It has been felt necessary to promote some exceptionalism and to calibrate those aspects of the doctrine of customary international law which frustrate the expansionist project.

245 Frédéric Mégret, 'International Human Rights Law Theory' available at SSRN: http://ssrn.com/abstract=1539591, at 20.

246 See the remarks of Koskenniemi, 'The Pull of the Mainstream' (n 63) 1947.

247 See d'Aspremont, *Formalism and the Sources of International Law* (n 4).

248 Simma and Alston, 'The Sources of Human Rights Law: Custom, Jus Cogens and General Principle' (n 63) 83.

249 Ibid 88, H. E. Chodosh, 'Neither Treaty nor Custom: The Emergence of Declarative International Law' (1991) 26 Texas International Law Journal 90, Louis Henkin, 'Human Rights and State "Sovereignty"' (1995–1996) 25 Georgia Journal of International and Comparative Law 37.

Examples of such exceptionalist use of custom for the sake of an expansionist discursivity are numerous.[250] It would be of no avail to review all their variants in detail. It suffices to say that such calibration commonly boils down to a greater focus on *opinio juris*,[251] the finding of practice in verbal statements,[252] the playing down of the requirement that any practice must be norm-creating to potentially crystallise in a customary norm,[253] or the reliance on deductive discursive moves.[254] Such exceptionalism echoes similar constructions

250 See e.g. Henkin, 'Human Rights and State "Sovereignty"' (n 99) 31, Meron, *Human Rights and Humanitarian Norms as Customary Law* (n 67) 88–89, Richard B. Lillich, 'The Growing Importance of Customary International Human Rights Law' (1995–1996) 25 Georgia Journal of International and Comparative Law 1, Jordan J. Paust, 'Complex, Nature, Sources and Evidences of Customary Human Rights' (1995) 25 Georgia Journal of International and Comparative Law 147, Arthur M. Weisburd, 'The Effect of Treaties and Other Formal International Acts on the Customary Law of Human Rights' (1995–1996) 25 Georgia Journal of International and Comparative Law 99, Jan Wouters and Cedric Ryngaert 'Impact on the Process of the Formation of Customary International Law' in M. Kamminga and M. Scheinin (eds.) *The Impact of Human Rights Law on General International Law* (Oxford University Press 2009) 111.

251 Wouters and Ryngaert 'Impact on the Process of the Formation of Customary International Law' (n 250).

252 Committee on Formation of Customary (General) International Law, 'Final Report on the Formation of Customary (General) International Law' (International Law Association, London 2000) 14.

253 This requirement was put forward by the ICJ in the case on the *North Sea Continental Shelf*. Indeed, on that occasion, the Court assessed the customary character of the equidistance principle enshrined in Article 6 of the 1958 Convention on the Continental Shelf and asserted that the norm at stake had first to be of a 'fundamentally norm-creating character such as could be regarded as forming the basis of a general rule of law'. The Court drew on the idea that any conventional rule must contain a directive for it to be able to one day crystallise into a customary international rule. Taking mainly into account the profound indeterminacy of the concept of 'special circumstances' which determines the qualification to the equidistance principle, the Court deemed that the principle of equidistance enshrined in the 1958 Convention was not normative. Because the principle of equidistance did not provide for a given behaviour to be adopted by the parties, the Court concluded that it could not crystallise or generate a rule of customary international law. See [1969] ICJ Rep. 1, at para. 72. See also the 3d Report of the Special Rapporteur of the ILC on identification of customary international law, 27 March 2015, A/CN.4/682, para. 39. For a discussion, see Jean d'Aspremont, 'Softness in International Law: A Self-Serving Quest for New Legal Materials' (2008) 19 European Journal of International Law 1075–1093.

254 See the work of the ILA Committee on International Human Rights Law and Practice, as reported by Kamminga, 'Final Report on the Impact of International Human Rights on General International Law', (n 112) 8.

witnessed with respect to customary international humanitarian law[255] which is largely reprised in the discourse on international human rights.[256]

Such exceptionalism has been extensively discussed and criticised in the literature.[257] It would be of no avail to revisit these debates here. What matters, for the sake of this book, is that such exceptionalism remains packaged in a generalist narrative whereby such exceptionalist moves are said to be consonant with the methodological rigour imposed by the general doctrine of customary international law as well as the case-law of the International Court of Justice.[258] In that sense, exceptionalism in relation to customary law is usually accompanied by a narrative that is very obedient to the traditional discursive constructions of general international law.[259] The extensive reliance

---

255 For an example of the loosening of the element of practice and more emphasis on opinion juris in international humanitarian law see ICTY, *Prosecutor v. Tadić* (Decision on the Defence Motion for Interlocutory Appeal on Jurisdiction) IT-94-1-AR72, (2 October 1995) para. 96–125; Jean-Marie Henckaerts and Louise Doswald-Beck, *Customary International Humanitarian Law*, Volume I: Rules (Cambridge 2006), xxxviii–xlii, Jean-Marie Henckaerts, 'Customary International Humanitarian Law: Taking Stock of the ICRC Study' (2009) 78 Nordic Journal of International Law 435–468. See Antonio Cassese, 'The Martens Clause: Half a Loaf or Simply Pie in the Sky?' (2000) 11 European Journal of International Law 187–216, esp. 213–215. For some critical remarks, see Jean d'Aspremont, 'An Autonomous Regime of Identification of Customary International Humanitarian Law: Do Not Say What You Do or Do Not Do What You Say?' in Raphaël van Steenberghe (ed.), *Droit International Humanitaire: Un Régime Spécial de Droit International?* (Bruylant 2013), available at SSRN: http://ssrn.com/abstract=2230345.

256 Wouters and Ryngaert 'Impact on the Process of the Formation of Customary International Law' (n 67) 116–118.

257 For a much-cited attempt to reconcile it, see Anthea Roberts, 'Traditional and Modern Approaches to Customary International Law: A Reconciliation' (2001) 95 American Journal of International Law 757.

258 See Meron, *Human Rights and Humanitarian Norms as Customary Law* (n 67) 81 and 247.

259 Such necessity to anchor exceptionalism into generalism can also manifest itself by the claim that their emancipatory moves are still respectful of state consent or even more respectful of state consent. See Wouters and Ryngaert 'Impact on the Process of the Formation of Customary International Law' (n 67) 111, 131. This presupposes that customary international law has always been an emanation of state consent, which seems to be a conception abandoned at the beginning of the 20th century. On the conventional foundations of customary law, see Heinrich Triepel, *Völkerrecht und Landesrecht* (Scientia Verlag 1899), Karl Strupp, *Elements du Droit International Public* (Rousseau 1927), Thomas Lawrence, *The Principles of International Law* (Macmillan 1915), John Westlake, *International Law* (Cambridge University Press 1904) 14, Dionisio Anzilotti, *Scritti di Diritto Internazionale Pubblico*, Vol 1 (Cedam 1957) 38, see also 95 ff. GI Tunkin, *Theory of International Law* (Harvard University Press 1974) 24. Charles Chaumont, 'Cours Général de Droit International Public', 129 Collected Courses (1970) 333, 440. For an attempt to modernise the consensual conception of customary international law, see Alexander Orakhelashvili, *The Interpretation of Acts and Rules in Public International Law* (Oxford

on the Nicaragua decision[260] to validate the greater emphasis placed on *opinio juris* particularly epitomises the extent to which international human rights law is permeated by a need to anchor its exceptionalism into general international law.[261] It is only rarely that they proudly trumpet their self-serving unorthodoxy.[262]

A few additional remarks are still warranted in order to grasp how custom serves the expansionist discursivity of international human rights law by wrapping exceptionalism into generalism. First, there is obviously no such a thing as a stable, fixed and objective doctrine of customary international law in general international law. That doctrine, which is – surprisingly[263] – derived from Article 38 of the Statute of the Permanent Court of International Justice has remained very unstable and indeterminate, continuously fuelling immense debates, as is illustrated by the work of the International Law Commission.[264] It is not even certain that a rigorously constructed argument could ever be

---

University Press 2008) 70–107, Anthony D'Amato, 'Treaties As a Source of General Rules of International Law' (1962) 3 Harvard International Law Journal 1–43. For some classic criticisms of such a convention-based approach to customary law, see Hersch Lauterpacht, 'Decisions of Municipal Courts as a Source of International Law' (1929) 10 British Yearbook of International Law, 65, 83, James Brierly, *The Law of Nations* (Clarendon Press 1955) 52, Josef Kunz, 'The Nature of Customary International Law' (1953) 47 American Journal of International Law 662, 664.

260 See *Nicaragua (Nicaragua v. United States of America)* (Merits) [1986], ICJ Rep. 14, 98, para. 184. See the remarks of Wouters and Ryngaert 'Impact on the Process of the Formation of Customary International Law' (n 67) 111, 112–115 and 123–124.

261 Wouters and Ryngaert 'Impact on the Process of the Formation of Customary International Law' (n 67) 111. See the work of the ILA Committee on International Human Rights Law and Practice, as reported by Kamminga, 'Final Report on the Impact of International Human Rights on General International Law', (n 112) 8, Meron, *Human Rights and Humanitarian Norms as Customary Law* (n 67) 106–114.

262 See e.g. Meron, *Human Rights and Humanitarian Norms as Customary Law* (n 67) 42, 68 and 74. See also Wouters and Ryngaert for whom it is uncontroversial that the more important the common interests of humanity, the greater weight may be attached to *opinio juris*. See Wouters and Ryngaert 'Impact on the Process of the Formation of Customary International Law' (n 67) 111.

263 Whilst it is traditionally assumed that the two-element theory is derived from article 38, it seems more convincing to contend that the two-element doctrine was a creation of the PCIJ rather than a creation of Article 38. See Christian Tams, *'Meta-Custom and the Court: A Study in Judicial Law-Making'*, (2015) 14 The Law and Practice of International Courts and Tribunals 54–57. See also Jean d'Aspremont, 'The Decay of Modern Customary International Law in Spite of Scholarly Heroism', (2016) 15 Global Community: Yearbook of International Law and Jurisprudence 9.

264 See the work of the ILC on the identification of customary international law. The various reports and conclusions are available at http://legal.un.org/ilc/guide/1_13.shtml.

made in relation to customary international law.[265] Second, even if the greater emphasis on *opinio juris* can be criticised as a departure from the traditional account and as a move towards deductivism and arbitrariness, it should be recalled that the element of state practice is not a more 'objective' criterion. Clearly, deriving a human rights norm from State practice would not be more 'objective'. Indeed, it has long been demonstrated that deriving norms from social facts such as state behaviour hinges on anterior choices about descriptive frameworks.[266] The same holds for practice under the doctrine of customary international law.[267] In that sense, establishing state practice is no less deductivist than establishing *opinio juris*.[268] Third, it seems difficult to deny that with respect to prohibitive norms like those generally contemplated under the international human rights law expansionist project, it is close to impossible to establish a practice of abstention, which is, by definition, highly intangible.[269] In that sense, the exceptionalism witnessed in relation to customary international human rights law would not necessarily need to be repackaged in a generalist discourse. Yet, scholarship and practice pertaining to customary international human rights law have shown the same inclination to present any emancipation from the general doctrine of customary international law as vindicated by general international law.

4.2 *General Principles of Law*

When the resort to customary international law to expand international human rights law does not seem possible, general principles of law, as they are envisaged by Article 38(1)(c) of the Statute of the International Court of

265 d'Aspremont, *Formalism and the Sources of International Law* (n 4), 162–170. See Jean d'Aspremont, 'Customary International Law as a Dance Floor – Part 1' (EJIL Talk), available at www.ejiltalk.org/customary-international-law-as-a-dance-floor-part-i/ and 'Customary International Law as a Dance Floor – Part 2' (EJIL Talk), available at www.ejiltalk.org/customary-international-law-as-a-dance-floor-part-ii/. In the same vein, Koskenniemi, 'The Pull of the Mainstream' (n 63) 1953.

266 It is a truism to say that descriptive frameworks are performative as they allow the construction of certain realities. See Alasdair McIntyre, *Whose Justice? Which Rationality?* (University of Notre Dame Press 1988) 333.

267 In the same vein, see Koskenniemi, 'The Pull of the Mainstream' (n 63) 1953.

268 See gen. William Worster, 'The Inductive and Deductive Methods in Customary International Law Analysis: Traditional and Modern Approaches' (2014) 45 Georgetown Journal of International Law 445.

269 See the remarks of Stefan Talmon, 'Determining Customary International Law: The ICJ's Methodology between Induction, Deduction and Assertion' (2015) 26 European Journal of International Law. This is maybe the only part of the (in)famous 1995 Tadić reasoning on customary law with which it seems possible to agree.

Justice, often seem to offer a plausible, albeit more limited, alternative. Indeed, a significant number of scholars have vindicated a central role for general principles of law for the further development of international human rights law.[270] It is probably no surprise that such expansionist use of general principles mostly constitutes a scholarly attitude. It is well known that international courts – subject to a few exceptions[271] – have generally been wary to rely on such a source of international law.[272] The reasons for such reservation probably lies in the open-endedness of the concept of general principles as well as the huge methodological problems associated with the extraction of common standards or mechanisms from various legal traditions which are most often incommensurable with one another.[273] Difficult and sensitive problems of sampling may have also deterred courts from engaging in an ascertainment of general principles. It is noteworthy that these difficulties have not dissuaded these international human rights law scholars, for whom general principles of law constitute an expansionist tool that had long been neglected.[274]

The contrast between those scholars' enthusiasm for general principles and the reservations of courts explains the exceptionalist character of the resort to general principles. The exceptionalism witnessed in this case is

---

270 See e.g. Simma and Alston, 'The Sources of Human Rights Law: Custom, Jus Cogens and General Principle' (n 63), Meron, *Human Rights and Humanitarian Norms as Customary Law* (n 67) 88, Hurst Hannum, 'The Status of the Universal Declaration of Human Rights in National and International Law' (1995–1996) 25 Georgia Journal of International and Comparative Law 287, 351–352, Wouters and Ryngaert 'Impact on the Process of the Formation of Customary International Law' (n 67) 111, 120–122, William Felice 'The Right to Development' in David Forsythe (ed.), *The Encyclopedia of Human Rights*, Vol. 2, (Oxford University Press 2009) 25.

271 E.g. the Inter-American Courts seems to have felt fewer qualms. See IACHR, Aloebeotoe et al, Reparations, Judgment of 19 September 1993, para. 62.

272 On the reluctance of the PCIJ and the ICJ to resort to general principles, see Pellet, 'Article 38' (n 67) 767, Gleider Hernandez, *The International Court of Justice and the Judicial Function* (Oxford University Press 2014) 261. When general principles have been referred to, they could hardly be distinguished from customary international law. See PCIJ, *Mavrommatis Palestine Concessions*, Judgment, PCIJ, Ser A, No. 5 (1925) at 30, PCIJ, *Factory at Chorzow* (*Germany v. Poland*), Merits, PCIJ Ser A No. 17 (1928), at 29, ICJ, Application for Review of Judgment No. 158 of the UN Administrative Tribunal, Advisory Opinion, 1973, ICJ Rep 166, 177, ICJ, *La Grand* (*Germany v. United States*), 2001 ICJ Rep 466, 503.

273 See Jaye Ellis, 'General Principles and Comparative Law' (2011) 22 European Journal of International Law 949–971. See also Koskenniemi, 'The Pull of the Mainstream' (n 63) 1948 and 1950.

274 For some criticisms of the use of general principles to develop IHRL, see Alain Pellet '"Human Rightism" and International Law', Gilberto Amado Memorial Lecture, 18 July 2000, 7.

different from the one observed in relation to customary international human rights law that has been discussed above. The scholarship about the use of general principles for the sake of the expansion of international human rights law is exceptionalist by virtue of its very use of general principles of law for expansionist purposes, rather than by virtue of how it deploys the legal categories associated by general principles, as they are commonly understood in the sources of international law.[275] Said differently, the exceptionalism in relation to general principles lies in the resurrection of a source of international law that has generally been neglected in the legal discourse, especially in the case-law.[276] Yet, like the exceptionalist posture noticed in relation to customary international human rights law, the exceptionalism pertaining to general principles is accompanied by a very generalist narrative. In the case of the expansionist use of general principles, such generalism materialises itself in claims that such a development of international human rights law is nothing more than the application of the general sources of international law or that it remains congruent with the consensual character of law-making.[277] Here too, one thus witnesses an expansionist approach to the sources that is nourished by both exceptionalist and generalist narratives. For instance, in the Corfu Channel Case the ICJ stated that the obligations of Albania were based "not on the Hague Convention (...) which is applicable in time of war, but on certain general and well-recognized principles, namely: elementary considerations of humanity".[278] Here the Court implicitly recognised that some general principles of international law were established to protect humanity.[279] In a

275 It is true that some proposed use of general principles may be less orthodox. See e.g. Wouters and Ryngaert 'Impact on the Process of the Formation of Customary International Law' (n 67) 111, 120–122.

276 In this respect, it is no surprise that some of the advocates of a use of general principles have been critical of the resort to customary rules. See Simma and Alston, 'The Sources of Human Rights Law: Custom, Jus Cogens and General Principle' (n 63) 96. For some critical remarks about general principles, see Jean d'Aspremont, 'What Was Not Meant to Be: General Principles of Law As a Source of International Law' in Riccardo Pisillo Mazzeschi and Pasquale De Sena (eds.), *Global Justice, Human Rights, and the Modernization of International Law* (Brill 2018).

277 Simma and Alston, 'The Sources of Human Rights Law: Custom, Jus Cogens and General Principle' (n 63) 107. It must be noted that these authors continue to hint at some kind of essentialism in their promotion of general principles as a tool to develop IHRL. See Simma and Alston, 'The Sources of Human Rights Law: Custom, Jus Cogens and General Principle' (n 63) 108 (referring to Louis Henkin).

278 ICJ, *Corfu Channel* (*United Kingdom v. Albania*), Judgment, 1949, ICJ Rep 4, at 22.

279 Simma and Alston, 'The Sources of Human Rights Law: Custom, Jus Cogens and General Principle' (n 63) 106.

similar vein, in the Advisory Opinion on the Genocide Convention the Court emphasised that the foundational principles of the Convention are binding on states regardless of any treaty obligation.[280]

4.3 *Soft Law*

It will not come as a surprise that when one has exhausted all avenues found in the traditional sources of international law, soft law comes as a last-resort technique to expand international human rights law.[281] The exceptionalism of such a move lies in the very fact that soft law, albeit enjoying some strong support in scholarship,[282] is usually not construed as a traditional source. And yet, it is used in the legal discourse on human rights to give a legal existence of some sort to those standards contemplated under human rights expansionist discursivity but not ascertainable through other sources of international law.[283] It will not come as a surprise that, here too, exceptionalism is accompanied by some generalist discourses which, for instance, may consist in seeking confirmation from the International Court of Justice that the standards concerned are legally relevant.[284] This is the case for example, when one examines the Nicaragua judgment where the Court analysed at length how the General Assembly resolutions can have normative value.[285]

4.4 *Other Source-Based Expansionist Moves*

Finally, mention must be made of a wide range of idiosyncratic constructions whereby new rules of international human rights law are discovered outside existing treaties. Although the use of such constructions remains

280 Reservations to the Genocide Convention (Advisory Opinion) [1951] ICJ Rep 15, para. 23. See also, Simma and Alston, 'The Sources of Human Rights Law: Custom, Jus Cogens and General Principle' (n 63) 106.

281 Michele Olivier, 'The Relevance of "Soft Law" as a Source of International Human Rights' (2002) 35 Comparative and International Law of Southern Africa 289, Catherine Turner, 'Human Rights and the Empire of (International) Law' (2011) 29 Law and Inequality 313, 331, Douglass Cassel, 'Inter-American Human Rights Law, Soft and Hard' in Dinah Shelton (ed.), *Commitment and Compliance: The Role of Non-Binding Norms in the International Legal System* (Oxford University Press 2000) 393–418.

282 See Jean d'Aspremont, 'Softness in International Law: A Self-Serving Quest for New Legal Materials' (2008) 19 European Journal of International Law, 1075–1093 and 'The Politics of Deformalization in International Law' (2011) 3 Goettingen Journal of International Law 503–550.

283 See e.g. Olivier (n 281) 289.

284 Turner (n 281) 331.

285 Military and Paramilitary Activities in and against Nicaragua (Nicaragua v United States), Merits, ICJ Reports 1986, para. 188–209.

a marginal scholarly phenomenon, a few of them are worthy of attention because they denote a similar oscillation between exceptionalism and generalism for the sake of expansionism. For instance, the expansion of international human rights law is sometimes promoted through arguments based on tacit acceptance[286] or universal consensus.[287] In the same vein, reference has been made to new obligations by virtue of implicit recognition.[288] The reconstruction of *jus cogens* into a source of international law rather than a limitation to the freedom to contract has similarly been invoked to expand international human rights law.[289] Equally creative has been the argument that, besides the traditional sources of international law, there exists other norm-creating processes supporting the creation of new rules of international human rights law. In this respect, references have been made to processes leading to the formal coalescence of demands of public conscience,[290] processes that include new law-making subjects[291] or processes said to be declarative of international human rights law.[292]

The exceptionalism of such constructions is not difficult to fathom. They conspicuously manifest some discursive extravagance in that they entail modes of law-ascertainment that are not found in the doctrine of the sources of international law. It is noteworthy, however, that they are all designed in a way that preserves some kinship with the main paradigms (or discursive moves) of general international law. They build on the existing structures

286 Meron, *Human Rights and Humanitarian Norms as Customary Law* (n 67) 89.

287 Antonio Cassese, 'The Geneva Protocols of 1977 on Humanitarian Law of Armed Conflict and Customary International Law' (1984) 3 UCLA Pasific Basin Law Journal 55, 113.

288 Oscar Schachter, 'International Law in Theory and Practice', 178 *Collected Courses* (1982-V) 335.

289 Wouters and Ryngaert 'Impact on the Process of the Formation of Customary International Law' (n 67) 120, Louis Henkin, 'Human Rights and State "Sovereignty"' (1995–1996) 25 Georgia Journal of International and Comparative Law 31, 383. On the special relationship between human rights and jus cogens, see the critical remarks of Andrea Bianchi, 'Human Rights and the Magic of Jus Cogens' (2008) 19 European Journal of International Law 491–508.

290 See G. Sperduti, *Lezioni di diritto internazionale* (1958), 68–74, as cited by Antonio Cassese, 'The Martens Clause: Half a Loaf or Simply Pie in the Sky?' (2000) 11 European Journal of International Law 187–216, 191.

291 Jordan J. Paust, 'Complex, Nature, Sources and Evidences of Customary Human Rights' (1995) 25 Georgia Journal of International and Comparative Law 147. See the remarks of Frédéric Mégret, 'International Human Rights Law Theory', available at SSRN: http://ssrn.com/abstract=1539591, at 21.

292 Hiram E. Chodosh, 'Neither Treaty nor Custom: The Emergence of Declarative International Law' (1991) 26 Texas International Law Journal 87.

of international law and employ narratives that come with some generalist overtones.[293] This is why, here too, one can find an exceptionalist approach to the sources of international human rights law packaged in a generalist narrative of some sort.

5 Possible Drivers of Expansionism in International Human Rights Law

The previous chapters have sought to show that expansionist constructions have been built on claims that oscillate between exceptionalist and generalist positions. The account offered in previous chapters has simultaneously shown the remarkable discursive creativity at work in international human rights law scholarship and practice. This chapter questions the motivations behind the expansionist discursivity and what might be gained from this expansionism. International human rights law expanded its scope by a constant oscillation between exceptionalist and generalist claims. This has allowed international human rights law to carve out its unique place within general international law while still preserving its connection with the latter. There are several possible reasons that drive this expansionist discursive practice. The following sections shed light on some of these drivers.

5.1 *Expansionism as a Managerial Mindset*

The creation of a special regime of international human rights law within general international law allows to establish a set of new interests and priorities to be protected by these special rules. Indeed, this is the case for any special regime within general international law. While international trade law highlights the priorities for the protection of the trade, international humanitarian law emphasises how civilians should be protected during an armed conflict. All special regimes will come up with their own list of values and underline the protection of a particular type of actor, theme or interest.[294] The creation of these special regimes allows to deploy a legal language to a problem in order to manage it through expert knowledge.[295] This allows to create a new legal

293 It is only rarely that bold – and even naturalistic – attempts to channel values into international law which cannot be reconciled with the sources of international law are vindicated. See e.g. Theodor Meron, 'The Martens Clause, Principles of Humanity, and Dictates of Public Conscience' (2000) 94 American Journal of International Law 78–89.

294 Martti Koskenniemi, 'The Politics of International Law–20 Years Later', (2009) 20 European Journal of International Law, 7–19, 11.

295 Koskenniemi, 'The Fate of Public International Law: Between Technique and Politics', (n 90).

vocabulary whereby human emancipation is carried out by bestowing rights to individuals and protecting them from the abuses of the state.[296] Rather than questioning how progressive change might take place when it comes to problems such as poverty, torture, censorship, racism or discrimination, this legal vocabulary created by the special regime of human rights turns these problems into legal problems and determines in which ways law can be involved in addressing them.

The creation of a special regime and the establishment of a set of new interests facilitate the creation of new problems that could easily be disregarded within general international law. International human rights law puts at its centre the individual, rather than the state or an international organisation, and then proceeds to construct new problems or make the existing problems relevant for this new set of rules. In that sense, the expansionism of international human rights law is closely linked with the belief that the problems of the world, including the protection of individual interests, preservation of international peace and security, protection of the environment can all be conceptualised as human rights problems. The managerial mindset allows to create a discourse of human rights that can be presented as a discourse of global emancipation.[297] Human rights can be seen as an easy getaway to bring solutions to world problems by turning them into human rights problems.[298] When the problems of the world are turned into human rights problems, this necessitates that these issues are resolved through a new set of rules. This requires a special regime that is sophisticated enough to respond to these problems. This managerialist approach is accompanied by the belief that the more rules we have, the more we can solve what we turned into human rights problems. In that regard, expansionism becomes a natural corollary of a managerialist approach to solving the problems of the world.[299]

296 David Kennedy, 'The International Human Rights Movement: Part of the Problem?', (2002) Harvard Human Rights Law Journal, 103–104, David Kennedy, 'The International Human Rights Regime: Still Part of the Problem', in Rob Dickinson et al. (eds.), *Examining Critical Perspectives on Human Rights* (Cambridge University Press 2012) 24.

297 Anthony J Langlois, 'Human Rights in Crisis? A Critical Polemic against Polemical Critics', (2012) 11 Journal of Human Rights, 558–70, 561.

298 David Kennedy, 'Reassessing International Humanitarianism: The Dark Sides' in Anne Orford (ed.), *International Law and Its Others* (Cambridge University Press 2006) 133–134.

299 Alston, 'Making Space for New Human Rights: The Case of the Right to Development', (n 16) 7.

5.2 *Expansionism as Rhetorical Power*

Expansionism is a discursivity that nourishes the rhetorical power of international human rights law. In parallel with the managerialist mindset, turning problems of the world into legal problems and generating a vocabulary unique to human rights helps to speak with the authority of general international law. Human rights that have long been part of philosophical discussions can decouple themselves from politics and morals once it gains a place within general international law. The authority to speak the legal language is bolstered by the expansionism that enriches the vocabulary which is at the disposal of anyone who wants to make use of this rhetorical power. International law allows human rights to speak the language of bindingness, enforcement, institutions, processes, rules, jurisprudence, precedents and implementation. Human rights, as part of international law, are no longer a set of moral codes but they are legal entitlements that dictate states how to treat their citizens and regulate their behaviour. They allow to make claims against the state with a legal vocabulary. In the same vein, Alston also noted that '[i]t is now widely accepted that the characterization of a specific goal as a human right elevates it above the rank and file of competing societal goals, gives it a degree of immunity from challenge and generally endows it with an aura of timelessness, absoluteness and universal validity.'[300] In other words, rather than arguing that something is morally unacceptable, it is more powerful to say that it constitutes a violation of human rights law.[301]

The more rules we have to proclaim what human rights are and how they should be protected, the more legal vocabulary one can produce to dominate the discourse. This specific language of human rights helps to create a new vocabulary to articulate specific needs and interests. The vocabulary of human rights grows through this expansionism and allows to put into words new demands. The expansionist discursivity can be used in that sense as a form of rhetorical power that strengthens the vocabulary by which these demands are formulated and put forward. For instance, human rights vocabulary harbours some strong expressions that can easily impress any audience. Universality, inalienability, indivisibility are some of the grand expressions that are very frequently used in any discourse about human rights and they are loaded with strong positive connotations. The language of human rights is inclusive and make use of expressions that come with convincing connotations. Even if

300 Ibid 3.

301 Romuald R. Haule, 'Some Reflections on the Foundation of Human Rights – Are Human Rights an Alternative to Moral Values?', (2006) 10 Max Planck Yearbook of United Nations Law 369.

it is accepted that words acquire a meaning in a specific context, when one refers to the universality of human rights or their indivisibility, the positive connotations that are usually associated with these words help to construct a persuasive narrative. The signifier in itself is a soothing material even before any meaning has been assigned to it. The context, what is meant, the interpretation of the expression might evade from the audience and in and of itself the use of the human rights vocabulary in a discourse can help to build a narrative of hope and justice.

International human rights law does not seem to be too much concerned with the end of grand narratives and builds its vocabulary on the authority of grand expressions.[302] International human rights law is universal, protects human dignity, equality and a long list of fundamental rights that can hardly be enumerated exhaustively. It has become in that sense a metadiscourse of justice. International human rights law has become such an important discourse that one of the reasons why the expansionist discursivity is welcomed without much hesitation is also due to the fear of its absence. Human rights seem self-evident and has a positive connotation. Its absence, non-enforcement, lack of respect seems to represent a natural cause of worry. It is also this fear of absence of human rights that becomes a motivating factor for more human rights and its expansionism. As a metadiscourse of justice, human rights have been so pervasive not only in legal sphere but also in everyday life, that its absence should be avoided at any cost.

An important grand expression that plays a significant role in the vocabulary of international human rights law is *jus cogens*. It is no coincidence that most norms that qualify as *jus cogens* are human rights norms. The prohibition of slavery, torture, genocide, racial discrimination are all part of the human rights vocabulary. While the positivisation of human rights is a strategic move to speak the language of law, rather than morals, the use of *jus cogens* in human rights discourse is as if morals were entering positive law through the back door in order to declare that some rights are more important than others.[303] The transformation of a norm into a *jus cogens* norm not only elevates it into a higher hierarchy compared to other ordinary norms but it further strengthens its rhetorical power.[304] While there might be justifications for the violation of general international law rules, this is not the case for some human rights

302 See generally, Jean-François Lyotard, *The Postmodern Condition: A Report on Knowledge* (University of Minnesota Press 1984).

303 Bianchi, 'Human Rights and the Magic of Jus Cogens', (n 289) 495.

304 Anthony d'Amato, 'It's a Bird, It's a Plane, It's Jus Cogens', (1990) 6 *Conneticut Journal of International Law* 1.

norms that qualify as *jus cogens*. The hierarchical superiority of these human rights norms is an important source of rhetorical power. The necessity of *jus cogens* has been discussed at length in the scholarship.[305] Suffice to note that by establishing a hierarchy between ordinary rules and rules of *jus cogens*, international human rights law benefit from the latter's non-derogable character to bestow a heightened importance to its discourse.

5.3 *Expansionism as Professional Sophistication*

When one constructs the problems of the world as human rights problems, this does not only create a special regime with its own values and priorities, but it further creates a new professional field. The sophistication of this special regime depends on the endeavour of those who take up the role of representing this field and working for its betterment. The sophistication of the field becomes part of a culture where those who work on this special regime commit themselves to the values that this culture represents.[306] The expansionism of international human rights law becomes not only a technique by which we can solve the world's problems, but also forms part of a professional identity and a belief in the problem-solving potential of the human rights expertise.[307] This eventually leads to the formation of a professional community of human rights lawyers who exclusively work on this special regime.

The creation of a special regime of international human rights law is simultaneously followed by the creation of a professional community of international human rights lawyers. When defending the values of human rights becomes a professional activity, this leads to the formation of a new epistemic community that works for the sophistication of this regime by producing expert

305 Robert Kolb, *Peremptory International Law-Jus Cogens: A General Inventory* (Bloomsbury Publishing 2015) 15–29, Alexander Orakhelashvili, *Peremptory Norms in International Law* (Oxford University Press 2006) 7–35, Dinah Shelton, 'Normative Hierarchy in International Law', (2006) 100 American Journal of International Law 291–323. Evan J Criddle and Evan Fox-Decent, 'A Fiduciary Theory of Jus Cogens', (2009) 34 *Yale Journal of International Law* 331, Ulf Linderfalk, 'The Effect of Jus Cogens Norms: Whoever Opened Pandora's Box, Did You Ever Think About the Consequences?', (2007) 18 European Journal of International Law, 853–71, Andreas Paulus, 'Jus Cogens in a Time of Hegemony and Fragmentation – an Attempt at a Re-Appraisal', (2005) 74 Nordic Journal of International Law, 297–333. See also ILC, 'Peremptory Norms of General International Law (Jus Cogens): Text of the Draft Conclusions and Draft Annex Provisionally Adopted by the Drafting Committee on First Reading', UN Doc CN.4/727 (2019).

306 Martti Koskenniemi, 'International Law: Constitutionalism, Managerialism and the Ethos of Legal Education', (2007) 1 *European Journal of Legal Studies*, 8, 10–11.

307 On the formation of a professional community of international lawyers, see Jean d'Aspremont, 'Professionalisation of International Law' in Jean d'Aspremont et al. (eds.), *International Law as a Profession* (Cambridge University Press 2017) 26–31.

knowledge.[308] This sophistication can be executed in two steps. First, it must be demonstrated how this special regime is different from general international law to gain a certain autonomy from the latter. It is only if international human rights law has different discursive constructions that it can ascertain its own distinct status within general international law. This is to that end that new discursive tools ought to be invented or that existing ones ought to be tailored to international human rights law. Second, in order to ensure that this special regime is sophisticated enough, the legal discourse has to be consolidated and armoured by new discursive tools. The richness of the human rights discourse can be seen as a sign of depth and therefore of sophistication.

5.4 *Expansionism as a Trump Card*

When international human rights law is emancipated from the discursive constructions of general international law, this can generate competing rules in both regimes. If there are two rules that regulate the same matter differently, in order to resolve a conflict between competing rules of the same hierarchy, one has to apply either the general principle of more specific rule prevails over more general rule (*lex specialis derogat legi generali*) or newer rule prevails over older rule (*lex posterior derogat legi priori*).[309] The general principle which dictates that the more specific rule may prevail over the more general rule becomes especially important in the relationship between general international law and international human rights law.[310] When there is a norm

---

308 On the relationship between human rights and epistemic communities, see generally David J Galbreath and Joanne Mcevoy, 'How Epistemic Communities Drive International Regimes: The Case of Minority Rights in Europe', (2013) 35 Journal of European Integration, 169–86, Peter Haas, 'International Environmental Law: Epistemic Communities', in Daniel Bodansky, Jutta Brunnée, and Ellen Hey (eds.), *The Oxford Handbook of International Environmental Law* (Oxford University Press 2012). See also, Andrea Bianchi, 'Epistemic Communities' in d'Aspremont and Singh (eds.), *Concepts for International Law: Contributions to Disciplinary Thought* (Edward Elgar 2019).

309 In relation to norm conflicts of a different hierarchy, see Marko Milanovic, 'Norm Conflict in International Law: Whither Human Rights', (2009) 20 Duke Journal of Comparative & International Law, 69, Bianchi, 'Human Rights and the Magic of Jus Cogens', (n 289), Alexander Orakhelashvili, *Peremptory Norms in International Law* (Oxford University Press 2006).

310 See International Law Commission, Report of the Working Group on Long-term Programme of Work, Risks Ensuing from the Fragmentation of International Law, ILC (LII)/WG/LT/L.1/Add. 1 (25 July 2000), 30–114. See also, The Gabcíkovo–Nagymaros Project (Hungary/Slovakia), ICJ Reports 1997, para. 132, Legality of the Threat or Use of Nuclear Weapons, Advisory Opinion, ICJ Reports 1996, para. 25, Legal Consequences of the Construction of a Wall in the Occupied Palestinian Territory, Advisory Opinion, ICJ Reports 2004, para. 102–113.

conflict between these two regimes, according to the main principle, if there is a more specific rule in international human rights law, it may prevail over a more general rule of international law. This is, however, possible if the rule of international human rights law is more specific than the one that it contradicts in general international law. This is a highly likely outcome since as a special regime of general international law, international human rights law regulates a much more specific field.

The general principle which dictates that the more specific rule may override the more general rule does not provide a straightforward answer in how the norm conflict should be resolved. The rationale of such a conflict resolution technique relies on the understanding that a more specific rule addresses the issue at hand with more effectiveness and clarity.[311] A more specific rule can equally be said to be more illustrative of state consent than a more general rule.[312] The principle establishes a priority rule which aims to determine which of the conflicting norms should be applied to the case at hand and is not concerned with the validity or legality of the norms in question.[313] In order to apply this principle, one has to establish which of the conflicting norms provides a more specific regulation. The determinant factor to establish which conflicting norm should be applied is the specificity of the norms in question. In other words, in case there is a conflict between a rule of international human rights law and general international law, one has to ascertain which one is *lex specialis*. This means that there is an inescapable battle between these two regimes when it comes to norm conflict. The rule that prevails will be determined based on the specificity of the said rules and this specificity will act as a trump card to override the more general rule. In so doing, the legal discourse ensures, not only that there are enough sources to cover a wide range of topics, but also that these sources are specific enough to prevail over general international law rules when there is a norm conflict. It is to the advantage of those who want international human rights rules to prevail over more general rules of international law to ensure that there is an abundant number of human rights sources addressing a wide range of topics that might not be covered by general international law. In that regard, expansionism becomes a useful tool to generate a trump card for international human rights law in a possible norm conflict with general international law.

311 ILC Study on Fragmentation, A/CN.4/L.682, 36, para. 60.

312 Joost Pauwelyn, *Conflict of Norms in Public International Law: How WTO Law Relates to Other Rules of International Law* (Cambridge University Press 2003) 388.

313 Ibid 327.

The principle of *lex specialis derogat generali* is an important reason for international human rights law to expand its sources to prevail over general international law. Expansionism becomes an essential manoeuvre to play the trump card, not only in the relationship between international human rights law as a special regime and general international law but also it becomes a useful tool in the relationship of the former with other special regimes. The literature on the clash between international human rights law and international humanitarian law and how norm conflicts can be resolved is abundant.[314] It suffices here to mention that it is a long disputed matter how the norm conflict between international human rights law which protects interests of individuals and international humanitarian law which protects those who take part in armed conflicts can be resolved. While it is generally accepted that international humanitarian law rules provide more specific regulations compared to international human rights law rules, and therefore constitute *lex specialis* in a possible clash, this does not mean that international human rights law loses all

314 Christian Tomuschat, 'Human Rights and International Humanitarian Law', (2010) 21 European Journal of International Law 15–23, Roberta Arnold and Noëlle Nr Quénivet (eds.), *International Humanitarian Law and Human Rights Law: Towards a New Merger in International Law* (Brill 2008), Marko Milanović, 'A Norm Conflict Perspective on the Relationship between International Humanitarian Law and Human Rights Law', (2009) 14 Journal of Conflict & Security Law 459–83, Robert Kolb and Gloria Gaggioli (eds.), *Research Handbook on Human Rights and Humanitarian Law* (Edward Elgar 2013), Jean-Marie Henckaerts and Ellen Nohle, 'Concurrent Application of International Humanitarian Law and International Human Rights Law Revisited', (2018) 12 Human Rights & International Legal Discourse 23, Françoise J Hampson, 'The Relationship between International Humanitarian Law and Human Rights Law from the Perspective of a Human Rights Treaty Body', (2008) 90/871 International Review of the Red Cross 549–72, Anthony E Cassimatis, 'International Humanitarian Law, International Human Rights Law, and Fragmentation of International Law', (2007) 56 International & Comparative Law Quarterly 623–39, Daniel Bethlehem, 'The Relationship between International Humanitarian Law and International Human Rights Law in Situations of Armed Conflict', (2013) 2 Cambridge International Law Journal 180–95, Marko Milanovic, 'The Lost Origins of Lex Specialis: Rethinking the Relationship between Human Rights and International Humanitarian Law', in Jens David Ohlin (ed.), *Theoretical Boundaries of Armed Conflict and Human Rights* (Cambridge University Press 2016), Alexander Orakhelashvili, 'The Interaction between Human Rights and Humanitarian Law: Fragmentation, Conflict, Parallelism, or Convergence?', (2008) 19 European Journal of International Law 161–82. See also, Legality of the Threat or Use of Nuclear Weapons, Advisory Opinion, ICJ Reports 1996, para. 25, Legal Consequences of the Construction of a Wall in the Occupied Palestinian Territory, Advisory Opinion, ICJ Reports 2004, para 106, Armed Activities on the Territory of the Congo (Democratic Republic of the Congo v. Uganda), Judgment, ICJ Reports 2005, para. 216.

relevance in the case of a norm conflict. There are two scenarios where expansionism of human rights sources can be useful to generate a trump card. While it is generally accepted that international humanitarian law regulates a more limited area and therefore constitutes *lex specialis* compared to international human right law, this does not mean that humanitarian law takes precedence without taking into account any other consideration. It is on a case by case basis, that one has to evaluate which one provides a more specific regulation. In case a human rights norm is more specific than a conflicting humanitarian norm, the former trumps the latter based on the principle of *lex specialis*. Indeed, if it is accepted that international law is fragmented and special regimes co-exist with their own rules, principles, processes and institutions, each special regime might clash with another special regime. In case there is a norm conflict, a special regime can prevail over another special regime, only if it provides a more specific rule. In other words, expansionism becomes an empowering tool that generates a trump card in the case of a norm conflict.

Further, it is generally accepted that international human rights law continues to apply during an armed conflict alongside international humanitarian law. This means that human rights norms can be used to interpret relevant humanitarian law rules or to substantiate them when there is a gap in a relevant norm.[315] In that sense, international human rights law does not only apply in case it provides a more specific regulation, but it might also apply alongside a humanitarian norm to help with the interpretation of a particular norm for systemic integration.[316] In that regard, expansionism becomes an efficient tool to ensure that there is a wide range of sources that can provide rules with enough specificity or rules that will fill the gaps of other special regimes and help with their interpretation.

5.5 *Expansionism as Discursive Proclivity*

It is often said that the development of international human rights law has played an essential role in raising individuals' living standards by strengthening domestic human rights protection mechanisms at the national level and establishing supranational bodies and courts to supervise the commitment of

315 Bethlehem, 'The Relationship between International Humanitarian Law and International Human Rights Law in Situations of Armed Conflict', (n 314) 188.

316 Jean d'Aspremont and Elodie Tranchez, 'The Quest for a Non-Conflictual Coexistence of International Human Rights Law and Humanitarian Law: Which Role for the Lex Specialis Principle?' in Kolb and Gaggioli (eds.), *Research Handbook on Human Rights and Humanitarian Law* (Edward Elgar 2013) 235–242.

states to international human rights obligations at the international level.[317] Such common image of international human rights law has buoyed a general belief that the proliferation of international human rights law is indeed a positive development that should not only be celebrated but also supported. In other words, since human rights can only do more good than harm, it can be claimed that there is no downside in having more human rights, an idea that nurtures the belief in the need for new discursive constructions to support the expansion of the reach of human rights. In that sense, expanding the sources of human rights law can be construed as a very central proclivity of the human rights discourse.[318] Due to the generally positive discourse that surrounds any debate on human rights, expansionism might seem self-evident. What might be wrong about creating more legal protection when it comes to rights that safeguard fundamental rights? There is almost an instinctive inclination to answer this question in the affirmative. It seems only natural to provide more protection to individuals against the possible abuses of their state. The expansionist discursivity can be interpreted as a discursive proclivity that aims to follow suit on the abovementioned belief with a view to possibly provide better protection for individuals' fundamental interests.

The origin of this discursive proclivity can be explained by various reasons. First, it should be underlined that the foundations of human rights predate its positivisation. It can be stated that human rights enjoyed strong and deep-rooted theoretical foundations in various fields, including politics,

317 On the relationship between human rights treaties and respect for human rights, see Samuel Moyn, 'Do Human Rights Make Enough of a Difference', in Conor Gearty and Costas Douzinas (eds.), *The Cambridge Companion to Human Rights Law* (Cambridge University Press 2012) 329, Eric Neumayer, 'Do International Human Rights Treaties Improve Respect for Human Rights?', (2005) 49 Journal of Conflict Resolution 925–53, Frank B Cross, 'The Relevance of Law in Human Rights Protection', (1999) 19 International Review of Law and Economics 87–98, Oona A Hathaway, 'Do Human Rights Treaties Make a Difference', (2002) 111 The Yale Law Journal 1935, Ryan Goodman and Derek Jinks, 'Measuring the Effects of Human Rights Treaties', (2003) 14 European Journal of International Law 171–83, Thomas Risse, Stephen C Ropp, and Kathryn Sikkink (eds.), *The Power of Human Rights: International Norms and Domestic Change* (Cambridge University Press 1999).

318 For a critical perspective, see Frédéric Mégret, 'Where Does the Critique of International Human Rights Stand? An Exploration in 18 Vignettes', in José María Beneyto et al. (eds.), *New Approaches to International Law* (Asser Press 2012), Antony Anghie, *Imperialism, Sovereignty and the Making of International Law* (Cambridge University Press 2007) 254–263, Balakrishnan Rajagopal, 'Counter-Hegemonic International Law: Rethinking Human Rights and Development as a Third World Strategy', (2006) 27 Third World Quarterly 767–83, Ratna Kapur, 'Human Rights in the 21st Century: Take a Walk on the Dark Side', (2006) 28 Sydney Law Review 665–87.

sociology, philosophy, religion, before it was transposed as a legal entitlement into international law.[319] It is only in the aftermath of the Second World War, following the adoption of the Universal Declaration of Human Rights that general international law started to be interested in the protection of individual interests through a legal vocabulary. Indeed, it is a very recent phenomenon that human rights have entered the international legal discourse. In that sense, it would be misleading to expect that human rights would cut all its connections with all these various fields once it was transposed into international instruments. In particular, the close connection of human rights with morals becomes a strong ideological driver for the expansionist proclivity of the human rights discourse. While the predominant approach would be to conceptualise international human rights as obligations that states consent to undertake, one can be easily inclined to accept that these are already pre-existing moral obligations. In that regard, it might be difficult to completely disregard the naturalist approach to the necessity of human rights.[320] It might seem counter-intuitive to think that states are bound by human rights principles only because they are party to a particular international human rights treaty. Human rights can easily be reflective of what one expects to find as protected by law from a moral perspective. As discussed in chapter 2, the relationship between morals and human rights has generated a rich literature. Here, it suffices to mention that according to some scholars, human rights are the legal replica of moral values.[321] Others argued that certain moral values are of such an importance that they deserve to be protected by the legal system.[322] The positivisation of human rights and their transformation into legal entitlements allowed these values to distance themselves from their moral premises and benefit from the authority of international law. This does not mean, however, that the positivisation of human rights breaks entirely any connection between these rights and their possible reflection in moral values. While the transformation of human rights into legal rights can help to move away from an approach that sees human rights merely as a moral code, the close relationship between morals and human rights continue to motivate those who aspire to expand this special regime.

319 Mégret, 'International Human Rights Law Theory' (n 94) 165.

320 Koskenniemi, 'The Pull of the Mainstream', (n 63) 1946–1947.

321 Joseph Raz, 'Human Rights without Foundations' (n 77) 321, Griffin, *On Human Rights* (n 77), Morsink, *The Universal Declaration of Human Rights: Origins, Drafting and Intent* (n 55).

322 Samantha Besson, 'Sources of International Human Rights Law: How General is General International Law' in Besson and d'Aspremont (eds.), *The Oxford Handbook of the Sources of International Law* (Oxford University Press 2016) 837.

5.6 *Expansionism as a Common Feature of Most Discourses*

A few observations ought to be offered on a final possible driver for the expansionism of international human rights law discussed in the previous chapters, these observations simultaneously offering some concluding thoughts on the discursive phenomenon discussed throughout this book. It is argued, at this concluding stage, that getting hold on new objects of thought and meaning-making and thus the creation of new discursive materials to which international human rights law can be applied may correspond to a pattern found in most discourses. Indeed, for discourses are ways to speak about the world, give it meaning, and organise it,[323] they can be seen as constantly seeking to conquer new terrains of thought and of meaning-making. Discourses would usually go on conquering new terrains of thought and of meaning-making through the *production of new discursive materials*[324] which are then immediately captured, organised, and ordered by the discourse concerned.[325] There is no reason why this should be different in the case of international human rights law. After all discourses move and define their boundaries strategically.[326] Such a feature of discourses can even be construed as an existential move, including for international human rights law. In fact, through an expansion of their terrains of thought and of meaning-making, discourses ensure their constant renewal and eternal relevance. In that sense, the expansionism of international human rights law that has been discussed in this book, is nothing more than the manifestation of a discourse working for itself.

---

323 See the definition of discourses, supra note 10.

324 Comp. with the idea of over-production of knowledge for the sake of ordering. see Michel Foucault, *Dits et écrits, II* (Gallimard 2001) 554–555. See also the idea of discursive eruption ('explosion discursive') see Michel Foucault, *Histoire de la Sexualité 1: La Volonté de Savoir* (Gallimard 1976) 25. The way in which an economy of secret serves a specific discourse ordering through an outpouring of discourse is at the heart of Michel Foucault's first volume on the history of sexuality. See gen. Michel Foucault, *Histoire de la Sexualité 1: La Volonté de Savoir* (Gallimard 1976), esp. 33, 48–49.

325 Michel Foucault, *Histoire de la Sexualité 1: La Volonté de Savoir* (Gallimard 1976) 48–49, Michel Foucault, *Dits et écrits, II* (Gallimard 2001) 248. On the idea of distinctions and binary categories as powerful modes of ordering, see Gilles Deleuze and Claire Parnet, *Dialogues* (Champs Essais 1996) 29, Roland Barthes, *Leçon* (Seuil 1978) 12, Bruno Latour, *Nous n'avons jamais été Modernes: Essai d'Anthropologie Symétrique* (La Découverte 1997) 68–69, Michel Foucault, *Les Mots et les Choses* (Gallimard 1966) 68–69. On the idea that thoughts classify and thus order, see Michel Foucault, *Naissance de la Clinique* (PUF 1963) 27.

326 On the idea that discourses exercise control over themselves, see Michel Foucault, L'ordre du Discours (Gallimard 1971) 23. Comp. with the idea that interpretive strategies do not come from the reader but from the interpretive community, see Stanley Fish, *Is There a Text in This Class?* (Harvard University Press 1980) 14.

Bibliography

Addo, Michael K (ed.), (2016), *International Law of Human Rights* (Routledge).

Ajevski, Marjan (2014), 'Fragmentation in International Human Rights Law – Beyond Conflict of Laws', *Nordic Journal of Human Rights*, 32 (2), 87–98.

Alston, Philip (1988), 'Making Space for New Human Rights: The Case of the Right to Development', *Harvard Human Rights Yearbook*, 1, 3.

Alston, Philip and Macdonald, Euan (eds.) (2008), *Human Rights, Intervention, and the Use of Force* (Oxford University Press).

Andenæs, Mads Tønnesson and Bjorge, Eirik (eds.) (2015), *A Farewell to Fragmentation* (Cambridge University Press).

Anghie, Antony (2007), *Imperialism, Sovereignty and the Making of International Law* (Cambridge University Press).

Anonymous (ed.), (1993), *Collected Courses of the Academy of the European Union Law, Vol. IV, 2* (Martinus Nijhoff Publishers).

Arnold, Roberta and Quénivet, Noëlle NR (eds.) (2008), *International Humanitarian Law and Human Rights Law: Towards a New Merger in International Law* (Brill).

Baderin, Mashood (2003), *International Human Rights and Islamic Law* (Oxford University Press).

Baratta, Roberto (2000), 'Should Invalid Reservations to Human Rights Treaties be Disregarded?', *European Journal of International Law*, 11 (2), 413–25.

Barthes, Roland (1978), *Leçon* (Seuil).

Bates, Ed (2008), 'Avoiding Legal Obligations Created by Human Rights Treaties', *International & Comparative Law Quarterly*, 57 (4), 751–88.

Bauman, Richard (2012), *Human Rights in Ancient Rome* (Routledge).

Beneyto, José María, et al. (eds.) (2012), *New Approaches to International Law* (Asser Press).

Besson, Samantha (2009), 'The Authority of International Law: Lifting the State Veil', *Sydney Law Review*, 31 (3), 343–80.

Besson, Samantha and Tasioulas, John (eds.) (2010), *The Philosophy of International Law* (Oxford University Press).

Besson, Samantha and d'Aspremont, Jean (eds.) (2017), *The Oxford Handbook of the Sources of International Law* (Oxford University Press).

Bethlehem, Daniel (2013), 'The Relationship between International Humanitarian Law and International Human Rights Law in Situations of Armed Conflict', *Cambridge International Law Journal*, 2 (2), 180–95.

Bianchi, Andrea (2008), 'Human Rights and the Magic of Jus Cogens', *European Journal of International Law*, 19 (3), 491–508.

Bianchi, Andrea, Peat, Daniel, and Windsor, Matthew (eds.) (2015), *Interpretation in International Law* (Oxford University Press).

Blick, Andrew (2015), *Beyond Magna Carta: A Constitution for the United Kingdom* (Oxford University Press).

Bodansky, Daniel, Brunnée, Jutta, and Hey, Ellen (eds.) (2012), *The Oxford Handbook of International Environmental Law* (Oxford University Press).

Buchanan, Allen (2013), *The Heart of Human Rights* (Oxford University Press).

Bourdieu, Pierre (1982), *Ce que Parler Veut Dire: L'économie des Echanges Linguistiques* (Fayard).

Bourguignon, Henry J (1988), 'The Belilos Case: New Light on Reservations to Multilateral Treaties', *Vanderbilt Journal of Transnational Law*, 29, 347.

Brems, Eva (2014), 'Should Pluriform Human Rights Become One? Exploring the Benefits of Human Rights Integration', *European Journal of Human Rights*, 447–70.

Brilmayer, Lea (2006), 'From 'Contract' to 'Pledge': The Structure of International Human Rights Agreements', *Yale Law School, Faculty Scholarship Series, Paper 3753*, available at https://openyls.law.yale.edu/handle/20.500.13051/3174.

Buchanan, Allen (2007), *Justice, Legitimacy, and Self-Determination: Moral Foundations for International Law* (Oxford University Press).

Buchanan, Allen (2011), 'Reciprocal Legitimation: Reframing the Problem of International Legitimacy', *Politics, Philosophy & Economics*, 10 (1), 5–19.

Buchanan, Allen (2013), *The Heart of Human Rights* (Oxford University Press).

Cannizzaro, Enzo (ed.), (2011), *The Law of Treaties Beyond the Vienna Convention: Essays in Honour of Giorgio Gaja* (Oxford University Press).

Cass, Deborah Z (2005), *The Constitutionalization of the World Trade Organization: Legitimacy, Democracy, and Community in the International Trading System* (OUP Catalogue).

Cassimatis, Anthony E (2007), 'International Humanitarian Law, International Human Rights Law, and Fragmentation of International Law', *International & Comparative Law Quarterly*, 56 (3), 623–39.

Charlesworth, Hilary (2002), 'International Law: A Discipline of Crisis', *The Modern Law Review*, 65 (3), 377–92.

Charlesworth, Hilary and Coicaud, Jean-Marc (eds.) (2010), *Fault Lines of International Legitimacy* (Cambridge University Press).

Charnovitz, Steve (2006), 'Nongovernmental Organizations and International Law', *American Journal of International Law*, 100 (2), 348–72.

Clapham, Andrew (2010), 'The Role of the Individual in International Law', *European Journal of International Law*, 21 (1), 25–30.

Costa, Jean-Paul (2011), 'On the Legitimacy of the European Court of Human Rights' Judgments', *European Constitutional Law Review*, 7 (2), 173–82.

Craven, Matthew (2000), 'Legal Differentiation and the Concept of the Human Rights Treaty in International Law', *European Journal of International Law*, 11 (3), 489–519.

Criddle, Evan J and Fox-Decent, Evan (2009), 'A Fiduciary Theory of Jus Cogens', *Yale Journal of International Law*, 34, 331.

Cross, Frank B (1999), 'The Relevance of Law in Human Rights Protection', *International Review of Law and Economics*, 19 (1), 87–98.

Cruft, Rowan, Liao, S Matthew, and Renzo, Massimo (eds.) (2015), *Philosophical Foundations of Human Rights* (Oxford University Press).

d'Aspremont, Jean (2011), *Formalism and the Sources of International Law: A Theory of the Ascertainment of Legal Rules* (Oxford University Press).

d'Aspremont, Jean (2012), 'Wording in International Law', *Leiden Journal of International Law*, 25 (3), 575–602.

d'Aspremont, Jean (2015), 'The Doctrine of Fundamental Rights of States and Anthropomorphic Thinking in International Law', *Cambridge International Law Journal*, 4 (3), 501–20.

d'Aspremont, Jean (2017), *International Law as a Belief System* (Cambridge University Press).

d'Aspremont, Jean (2021), *The Discourse on Customary International Law* (Oxford University Press).

d'Aspremont, Jean (2021), *After Meaning: The Sovereignty of Forms in International Law* (Edward Elgar).

d'Aspremont, Jean (2022), 'Two Attitudes toward Textuality in International Law: The Battle for Dualism', 42 Oxford Journal of Legal Studies 963–984.

d'Aspremont, Jean (2023), 'The Love for International Organizations', 20 International Organizations Law Review 111–159.

d'Aspremont, Jean (2023), 'The Chivalric Pursuit of Coherence in International Law", 36 Leiden Journal of International Law (forthcoming).

d'Aspremont, Jean, et al. (eds.) (2017), *International Law as a Profession* (Cambridge University Press).

d'Amato, Anthony (1990), 'It's a Bird, It's a Plane, It's Jus Cogens', *Conneticut Journal of International Law*, 6, 1.

d'Aspremont, Jean and Singh, Sahib (eds.) (2019), *Concepts for International Law: Contributions to Disciplinary Thought* (Edward Elgar).

De Wet, Erika (2006), 'The International Constitutional Order', *International & Comparative Law Quarterly*, 55 (1), 51–76.

Delbrück, Jost (1992), 'A Fresh Look at Humanitarian Intervention under the Authority of the United Nations', *Indiana Law Journal*, 67, 887.

Deleuze, Gilles, Claire Parnet (1996), *Dialogues* (Champs Essais).

Derrida, Jacques (2011), *The Beast and the Sovereign*, vol 1 (University of Chicago Press).

Derrida, Jacques (2001), *Papier Machine* (Galilée).

Dickinson, Rob, et al. (eds.) (2012), *Examining Critical Perspectives on Human Rights* (Cambridge University Press).

Dörr, Oliver and Schmalenbach, Kirsten (eds.) (2018), *Vienna Convention on the Law of Treaties: A Commentary* (Springer).

Douzinas, Costas (2000), *The End of Human Rights: Critical Thought at the Turn of the Century* (Oxford University Press).

Dunoff, Jeffrey L (2006), 'Constitutional Conceits: The WTO's 'Constitution'and the Discipline of International Law', *European Journal of International Law*, 17 (3), 647–75.

Dunoff, Jeffrey L and Trachtman, Joel P (eds.) (2009), *Ruling the world?: constitutionalism, international law, and global governance* (Cambridge University Press).

Dupuy, Pierre-Marie (1997), 'The Constitutional Dimension of the Charter of the United Nations Revisited', *Max Planck Yearbook of United Nations Law Online*, 1 (1).

Evans, Malcolm (ed.), (2018), *International Law* (Oxford University Press).

Evatt, Elizabeth (1999), 'Democratic People's Republic of Korea and the ICCPR: Denunciation as an Exercise of the Right of Self-Defence?', *Australian Journal of Human Rights*, 5 (1), 215–24.

Fassbender, Bardo (1998), 'The United Nations Charter as Constitution of the International Community', *Columbia Journal of Transnational Law*, 36, 529.

Fastenrath, Ulrich et al. (eds.) (2011), *From Bilateralism to Community Interest: Essays in Honour of Bruno Simma* (Oxford University Press).

Fisher, Eran, (2010), *Media and New Capitalism in the Digital Age* (Palgrave Macmillan).

Fleck, Dieter (ed.), (2021), *The Handbook of International Humanitarian Law* (Oxford University Press).

Follesdal, Andreas (2017), 'Exporting the Margin of Appreciation: Lessons for the Inter-American Court of Human Rights', *International Journal of Constitutional Law*, 15 (2), 359–71.

Forsythe, David P (ed.), (2009), *Encyclopedia of Human Rights* (Oxford University Press).

Foucault, Michel (1971), *L'ordre du Discours* (Gallimard).

Foucault, Michel (2001), *Dits et écrits, Tome 2* (Gallimard).

Foucault, Michel (1976), *Histoire de la Sexualité 1: La Volonté de Savoir* (Gallimard).

Foucault, Michel (1966), *Les Mots et les Choses* (Gallimard).

Foucault, Michel (1963), *Naissance de la Clinique* (PUF).

Foucault, Michel (2004), *Sécurité, Territoire, Population: Cours au Collège de France, 1977–1978* (Gallimard).

Galbreath, David J and McEvoy, Joanne (2013), 'How Epistemic Communities Drive International Regimes: The Case of Minority Rights in Europe', *Journal of European Integration*, 35 (2), 169–86.

Gardbaum, Stephen (2008), 'Human Rights as International Constitutional Rights', *European Journal of International Law*, 19 (4), 749–68.

Gardner, JP (ed.), (1997), *Human Rights as General Norms and a State's Right to Opt Out: Reservations and Objections to Human Rights Conventions* (British Institute of International and Comparative Law).

Gearty, Conor and Douzinas, Costas (eds.) (2012), *The Cambridge Companion to Human Rights Law* (Cambridge University Press).

Glendon, Mary Ann (2002), *A World Made New: Eleanor Roosevelt and the Universal Declaration of Human Rights* (Random House).

Goodman, Ryan and Jinks, Derek (2003), 'Measuring the Effects of Human Rights Treaties', *European Journal of International Law*, 14 (1), 171–83.

Gourgourinis, Anastasios (2011), 'General/Particular International Law and Primary/ Secondary Rules: Unitary Terminology of a Fragmented System', *European Journal of International Law*, 22 (4), 993–1026.

Griffin, James (2009), *On Human Rights* (Oxford University Press).

Hampson, Françoise J (2008), 'The Relationship between International Humanitarian Law and Human Rights Law from the Perspective of a Human Rights Treaty Body', *International Review of the Red Cross*, 90 (871), 549–72.

Hannum, Hurst (1995), 'The Status of the Universal Declaration of Human Rights in National and International Law', *Georgia Journal of International and Comparative Law*, 25, 287.

Hathaway, Oona A (2002), 'Do Human Rights Treaties Make a Difference', *The Yale Law Journal*, 111, 1935.

Helfer, Laurence (2005), 'Exiting Treaties', *Virginia Law Review*, 91, 1579.

Helfer, Laurence R (2003), 'Constitutional Analogies in the International Legal System', *Loyola of Los Angeles Law Review*, 37, 193.

Henckaerts, Jean-Marie and Nohle, Ellen (2018), 'Concurrent Application of International Humanitarian Law and International Human Rights Law Revisited', *Human Rights & International Legal Discourse*, 12, 23.

Henkin, Louis (1978), 'Constitutional rights and human rights', *Harvard Civil Rights-Civil Liberties Law Review*, 13, 633.

Henkin, Louis (1995), 'Human Rights and State Sovereignty', *Georgia Journal of International and Comparative Law*, 25, 31.

Henkin, Louis (1999), 'That S Word: Sovereignty, and Globalization, and Human Rights, et cetera', *Fordham Law Review*, 68, 1.

Hernández, Gleider (2014), *The International Court of Justice and the Judicial Function* (Oxford University Press).

Higgins, Rosalyn (1978), 'Conceptual Thinking about the Individual in International Law', *British Journal of International Studies*, 4 (1), 1–19.

Higgins, Rosalyn (1989), 'Human Rights: Some Questions of Integrity', *Commonwealth Law Bulletin*, 15 (2), 598–614.

Higgins, Rosalyn (1995), *Problems and process: international law and how we use it* (Oxford University Press).

Hollis, Duncan et al (eds.) (2012), *The Oxford Guide to Treaties* (Oxford University Press).

Hunt, Lynn (2008), *Inventing Human Rights: A History* (WW Norton & Company).

Hylton, Daniel N (1994), 'Default Breakdown: The Vienna Convention on the Law of Treaties' Inadequate Framework on Reservations', *Vanderbilt Journal of Transnational Law*, 27, 419.

Ishay, Micheline (2008), *The History of Human Rights: From Ancient Times to the Globalization Era* (University of California Press).

Kammerhofer, Jörg and d'Aspremont, Jean (eds.) (2014), *International Legal Positivism in a Post-Modern World* (Cambridge University Press).

Kamminga, Menno and Scheinin, Martin (eds.) (2009), *The Impact of Human Rights law on General International Law* (Oxford University Press).

Kamminga, Menno T (1996), 'State Succession in Respect of Human Rights Treaties', *European Journal of International Law*, 7, 469.

Kapur, Ratna (2006), 'Human Rights in the 21st Century: Take a Walk on the Dark Side', *Sydney Law Review*, 28 (4), 665–87.

Kennedy, David (1986), 'Critical Theory, Structuralism and Contemporary Legal Scholarship' (1985–1986) 21 New England Law Review 209.

Kennedy, David (1987), 'The Move to Institutions', *Cardozo Law Review*, 8, 841–988.

Kennedy, David (1994), 'The International Style in Postwar Law and Policy', *Utah Law Review*, 7–103.

Kennedy, David (2002), 'The International Human Rights Movement: Part of the Problem?', *Harvard Human Rights Law Journal*.

Kennedy, David (2005), *The Dark Sides of Virtue: Reassessing International Humanitarianism* (Princeton University Press).

Klabbers, Jan (1997), 'Some Problems Regarding the Object and Purpose of Treaties', *Finnish Yearbook of International Law*, 8, 138–60.

Klabbers, Jan (2004), 'Constitutionalism Lite', *International Organizations Law Review*, 1 (1), 31–58.

Klabbers, Jan (2015), 'The EJIL Foreword: The Transformation of International Organizations Law', *European Journal of International Law*, 26 (1), 9–82.

Klabbers, Jan, Peters, Anne, and Ulfstein, Geir (2009), *The Constitutionalization of International Law* (Oxford University Press).

Kleinlein, Thomas (2019), 'The Procedural Approach of the European Court of Human Rights: Between Subsidiarity and Dynamic Evolution', *International & Comparative Law Quarterly*, 68 (1), 91–110.

Klug, Francesca (2015), *A Magna Carta for All Humanity: Homing in on Human Rights* (Routledge).

Kolb, Robert (2006), 'Principles as Sources of International Law (with Special Reference to Good Faith)', *Netherlands International Law Review*, 53 (1), 1–36.

Kolb, Robert (2015), *Peremptory International Law-Jus Cogens: A General Inventory* (Bloomsbury Publishing).

Kolb, Robert and Gaggioli, Gloria (eds.) (2013), *Research Handbook on Human Rights and Humanitarian Law* (Edward Elgar).

Koskenniemi, Martti (1990a), 'The Pull of the Mainstream', *Michigan Law Review*, 88, 1946–62.

Koskenniemi, Martti (1990b), 'The Politics of International Law', *European Journal of International Law*, 1, 4.

Koskenniemi, Martti (2006a), 'Constitutionalism as Mindset: Reflections on Kantian Themes about International Law and Globalization', *Theoretical Inquiries in Law*, 8 (1), 9–36.

Koskenniemi, Martti (2006b), *From Apology to Utopia: The Structure of international legal argument* (Cambridge University Press).

Koskenniemi, Martti (2007a), 'International Law: Constitutionalism, Managerialism and the Ethos of Legal Education', *European Journal of Legal Studies*, 1, 8.

Koskenniemi, Martti (2007b), 'The Fate of Public International Law: Between Technique and Politics', *The Modern Law Review*, 70 (1), 1–30.

Koskenniemi, Martti (2009), 'The Politics of International Law–20 Years Later', *European Journal of International Law*, 20 (1), 7–19.

Koskenniemi, Martti and Leino, Päivi (2002), 'Fragmentation of international law? Postmodern Anxieties', *Leiden Journal of International Law*, 15 (3), 553–79.

Kratochvíl, Jan (2011), 'The Inflation of the Margin of Appreciation by the European Court of Human Rights', *Netherlands Quarterly of Human Rights*, 29 (3), 324–57.

Krisch, Nico (2010), *Beyond Constitutionalism: The Pluralist Structure of Postnational Law* (Oxford University Press).

Langlois, Anthony J (2012), 'Human Rights in Crisis? A Critical Polemic Against Polemical Critics', *Journal of Human Rights*, 11 (4), 558–70.

Lauterpacht, Hersch (1950), *International Law and Human Rights* (Stevens).

Lemke, Jay (2001), 'Discursive Technologies and the Social Organization of Meaning', 35 Folia Linguistica, 79–96.

Lemke, Jay (first ed. 1945, 2013), *An International Bill of Rights of Man* (Oxford University Press).

Lijnzaad, Elizabeth (1995), *Reservations to UN-Human Rights Treaties: Ratify and Ruin?* (Martinus Nijhoff Publishers).

Linderfalk, Ulf (2007), 'The Effect of Jus Cogens Norms: Whoever Opened Pandora's Box, Did You Ever Think About the Consequences?', *European Journal of International Law*, 18 (5), 853–71.

Lindroos, Anja (2005), 'Addressing Norm Conflicts in a Fragmented Legal System: The Doctrine of Lex Specialis', *Nordic Journal of International Law*, 74 (1), 27–66.

Lyotard, Jean-François (1984), *The Postmodern Condition: A Report on Knowledge* (University of Minnesota Press).

Macklem, Patrick (2015), *The Sovereignty of Human Rights* (Oxford University Press).

Mahoney, Jack (2008), *The Challenge of Human Rights: Origin, Development and Significance* (Wiley-Blackwell).

Martineau, Anne-Charlotte (2009), 'The Rhetoric of Fragmentation: Fear and Faith in International Law', *Leiden Journal of International Law*, 22 (1), 1–28.

Martinez, Jenny S (2011), *The Slave Trade and the Origins of International Human Rights Law* (Oxford University Press).

McCall-Smith, Kasey L (2014), 'Severing Reservations', *International & Comparative Law Quarterly*, 63 (3), 599–634.

McLachlan, Campbell (2005), 'The Principle of Systemic Integration and Article 31 (3)(c) of the Vienna Convention', *International & Comparative Law Quarterly*, 54 (2), 279–320.

Meron, Theodor (1986), *Human Rights Law-Making in the United Nations: A Critique of Instruments and Process* (Oxford University Press).

Meron, Theodor (1989), *Human Rights and Humanitarian Norms as Customary Law* (Oxford University Press).

Meron, Theodor (2006), *The Humanization of International Law* (Martinus Nijhoff Publishers).

Milanovic, Marko (2009), 'Norm Conflict in International Law: Whither Human Rights', *Duke Journal of Comparative & International Law*, 20, 69.

Milanović, Marko (2009), 'A Norm Conflict Perspective on the Relationship between International Humanitarian Law and Human Rights Law', *Journal of Conflict & Security Law*, 14 (3), 459–83.

Moeckli, Daniel, et al. (eds.) (2014), *International Human Rights Law* (Oxford University Press).

Moïse Mbengue, Makane and d'Aspremont, Jean (eds.) (2021), *Crisis Narratives in International Law* (Brill).

Morsink, Johannes (1999), *The Universal Declaration of Human Rights: Origins, Drafting and Intent* (University of Pennsylvania Press).

Mowbray, Alastair (2015), 'Subsidiarity and the European Convention on Human Rights', *Human Rights Law Review*, 15 (2), 313–41.

Moyn, Samuel (2012), *The Last Utopia: Human Rights in History* (Harvard University Press).

Murphy, Liam (2014), *What Makes Law: An Introduction to the Philosophy of Law* (Cambridge University Press).

Mutua, Makau (1996), 'The Ideology of Human Rights', *Virginia Journal of International Law*, 36, 589–658.

Mutua, Makau (2001), 'Savages, Victims, and Saviors: The Metaphor of Human Rights', *Harvard International Law Journal*, 42, 201.

Neuman, Gerald L (2002), 'Human Rights and Constitutional Rights: Harmony and Dissonance', *Stanford Law Review*, 55, 1863.

Neuman, Gerald L (2008), 'Import, Export, and Regional Consent in the Inter-American Court of Human Rights', *European Journal of International Law*, 19 (1), 101–23.

Neumayer, Eric (2005), 'Do International Human Rights Treaties Improve Respect for Human Rights?', *Journal of Conflict Resolution*, 49 (6), 925–53.

Neumayer, Eric (2007), 'Qualified Ratification: Explaining Reservations to International Human Rights Treaties', *The Journal of Legal Studies*, 36 (2), 397–429.

Ohlin, Jens David (ed.), (2016), *Theoretical Boundaries of Armed Conflict and Human Rights* (Cambridge University Press).

Oppenheim, Lassa (2018), *International Law: A Treatise, Volume 1* (Longmans).

Orakhelashvili, Alexander (2000), 'The Position of the Individual in International Law', *California Western International Law Journal*, 31, 241.

Orakhelashvili, Alexander (2006), *Peremptory Norms in International Law* (Oxford University Press).

Orakhelashvili, Alexander (2008), 'The Interaction between Human Rights and Humanitarian Law: Fragmentation, Conflict, Parallelism, or Convergence?', *European Journal of International Law*, 19 (1), 161–82.

Orakhelashvili, Alexander (ed.), (2020), *Research Handbook on the Theory and History of International Law* (Edward Elgar).

Orford, Anne (ed.), (2006), *International Law and its Others* (Cambridge University Press).

Parlett, Kate (2011), *The Individual in the International Legal System: Continuity and Change in International Law* (Cambridge University Press).

Paulus, Andreas (2005), 'Jus Cogens in a Time of Hegemony and Fragmentation – An Attempt at a Re-appraisal', *Nordic Journal of International Law*, 74 (3–4), 297–333.

Pauwelyn, Joost (2003), *Conflict of Norms in Public International Law: How WTO Law Relates to Other Rules of International Law* (Cambridge University Press).

Paveau, Marie-Anne (2006), 'Les Prédiscours: Sens, Mémoire, Cognition, Presses Sorbonne Nouvelle 132.

Peters, Anne (2016), *Beyond Human Rights: The Legal Status of the Individual in International Law* (Cambridge University Press).

Petersmann, Ernst-Ulrich (2000), 'The WTO Constitution and Human Rights', *Journal of International Economic Law*, 3 (1), 19–25.

Pogge, Thomas (1989), *Realizing Rawls* (Cornell University Press).

Prost, Mario (2012), *The Concept of Unity in Public International Law* (Bloomsbury Publishing).

Rajagopal, Balakrishnan (2006), 'Counter-Hegemonic International Law: Rethinking Human Rights and Development as a Third World Strategy', *Third World Quarterly*, 27, 767–83.

Redgwell, Catherine (1993), 'Universality or Integrity? Some Reflections on Reservations to General Multilateral Treaties', *British Yearbook of International Law*, 64 (1), 245–82.

Redgwell, Catherine (1997), 'Reservations to Treaties and Human Rights Committee General Comment No. 24 (52)', *International & Comparative Law Quarterly*, 46 (2), 390–412.

Reisman, W Michael (1990), 'Sovereignty and Human Rights in Contemporary International Law', *American Journal of International Law*, 84 (4), 866–76.

Reus-Smit, Christian (2001), 'Human Rights and the Social Construction of Sovereignty', *Review of International Studies*, 27 (4), 519–38.

Risse, Thomas, Ropp, Stephen C, and Sikkink, Kathryn (eds.) (1999), *The Power of Human Rights: International Norms and Domestic Change* (Cambridge University Press).

Rodgers, Gerry, et al. (2009), *The International Labour Organization and the Quest for Social Justice, 1919–2009* (International Labour Office).

Saunders, Imogen (2021), *General Principles as a Source of International Law: Art 38 (1)(c) of the Statute of the International Court of Justice* (Bloomsbury Publishing).

Schabas, William (1995), 'Reservations to Human Rights Treaties: Time for Innovation and Reform', *Canadian Yearbook of International Law* 32.

Schwöbel, Christine EJ (2011), *Global Constitutionalism in International Legal Perspective* (Brill).

Shaw, Malcolm N (2014), *International Law* (Cambridge University Press).

Sheeran, Scott and Rodley, Nigel (eds.) (2014), *Routledge Handbook of International Human Rights Law* (Routledge).

Shelton, Dinah (2005), *Remedies in International Human Rights Law* (Oxford University Press).

Shelton, Dinah (2006), 'Normative Hierarchy in International Law', *American Journal of International Law*, 100 (2), 291–323.

Shelton, Dinah (ed.), (2013), *The Oxford Handbook of International Human Rights Law* (Oxford University Press).

Sicilianos, Linos-Alexander (1993), 'The Relationship between Reprisals and Denunciation or Suspension of a Treaty', *European Journal of International Law*, 4, 341.

Simma, Bruno (1985), 'Self-Contained Regimes', *Netherlands Yearbook of International Law*, 16, 111–36.

Simma, Bruno (2009), 'Universality of International Law from the Perspective of a Practitioner', *European Journal of International Law*, 20 (2), 265–97.

Simma, Bruno and Alston, Philip (1988), 'The Sources of Human Rights Law: Custom, Jus Cogens, and General Principles', *Australian Yearbook of International Law*, 12, 82.

Simma, Bruno and Pulkowski, Dirk (2006), 'Of Planets and the Universe: Self-Contained Regimes in International Law', *European Journal of International Law*, 17 (3), 483–529.

Singh, Sahib (2011), 'The Potential of International Law: Fragmentation and Ethics', *Leiden Journal of International Law*, 24 (1), 23–43.

Slotte, Pamela and Halme, Miia (eds.) (2015), *Revisiting the Origins of Human Rights* (Cambridge University Press).

Somek, Alexander (2007), 'Kelsen Lives', *European Journal of International Law*, 18 (3), 409–51.

Somek, Alexander (2009), 'The Concept of 'Law'in Global Administrative Law: A Reply to Benedict Kingsbury', *European Journal of International Law*, 20 (4), 985–95.

Spano, Robert (2014), 'Universality or Diversity of Human Rights? Strasbourg in the Age of Subsidiarity', *Human Rights Law Review*, 14 (3), 487–502.

Spano, Robert (2018), 'The Future of the European Court of Human Rights – Subsidiarity, Process-Based Review and the Rule of Law', *Human Rights Law Review*, 18 (3), 473–94.

Spielmann, Dean (2012), 'Allowing the Right Margin: The European Court of Human Rights and the National Margin of Appreciation Doctrine: Waiver or Subsidiarity of European Review?', *Cambridge Yearbook of European Legal Studies*, 14, 381–418.

Sweet, Alec Stone (2009), 'Constitutionalism, Legal Pluralism, and International Regimes', *Indiana Journal of Global Legal Studies*, 16 (2), 621–45.

Tams, Christian (2005), *Enforcing Obligations Erga Omnes in International Law* (Cambridge University Press).

Tams, Christian and Tzanakopoulos, Antonios (eds.) (2014), *Research Handbook on the Law of Treaties* (Edward Elgar).

Tomuschat, Christian (2010), 'Human Rights and International Humanitarian Law', *European Journal of International Law*, 21 (1), 15–23.

Tsagourias, Nicholas (ed.), (2007), *Transnational Constitutionalism: International and European Perspectives* (Cambridge University Press).

Tyagi, Yogesh (2001), 'The Conflict of Law and Policy on Reservations to Human Rights Treaties', *The British Year Book of International Law*, 71 (1), 181.

Tyagi, Yogesh (2009), 'The Denunciation of Human Rights Treaties', *The British Year Book of International Law*, 79 (1), 86.

Unger, Roberto Mangabeira (1976), *Knowledge and Politics* (Free Press).

van Dijk, Boyd (2022), *Preparing for War: The Making of the 1949 Geneva Conventions* (Oxford University Press).

Walter, Christian (2001), 'Constitutionalizing (Inter)national Governance-Possibilities for and Limits to the Development of an International Constitutional Law', *German Yearbook of International Law*, 44, 170.

Weatherley, Robert (1999), *The Discourse of Human Rights in China: Historical and Ideological Perspectives* (Springer).

Weiler, Joseph (2004), 'The Geology of International Law: Governance, Democracy and Legitimacy', *ZAÖRV*, 46, 547–62.

White, James Boyd (1985), *The Legal Imagination* (University of Chicago Press).

White, James Boyd (1978), *Tropics of Discourse: Essays in Cultural Criticism* (Johns Hopkins University Press).

Wood, Michael (2013), 'Institutional Aspects of the Guide to Practice on Reservations', *European Journal of International Law*, 24 (4), 1099–112.

Ziemele, Ineta and Liede, Lāsma (2013), 'Reservations to Human Rights Treaties: From Draft Guideline 3.1. 12 to Guideline 3.1. 5.6', *European Journal of International Law*, 24 (4), 1135–52.

Ziemele, Ineta (ed.), (2004), *Reservations to Human Rights Treaties and the Vienna Convention Regime: Conflict, Harmony or Reconciliation* (Martinus Nijhoff Publishers).

Zimmermann, Andreas, et al. (eds.) (2019), *The Statute of the International Court of Justice: A Commentary* (Oxford University Press).

www.ingramcontent.com/pod-product-compliance
Lightning Source LLC
Chambersburg PA
CBHW031329230926
51848CB00001B/161
9789004696075